LEADERSHIP
in the HOOD

Talking about leadership application and
management issues in organisations

BOB SUTTON

BALBOA
PRESS

A DIVISION OF HAY HOUSE

Balboa Press books may be ordered through booksellers or by contacting:

Balboa Press
A Division of Hay House
1663 Liberty Drive
Bloomington, IN 47403
www.balboapress.com.au
1 (877) 407-4847

Because of the dynamic nature of the Internet, any web addresses or links contained in this book may have changed since publication and may no longer be valid. The views expressed in this work are solely those of the author and do not necessarily reflect the views of the publisher, and the publisher hereby disclaims any responsibility for them.

The author of this book does not dispense medical advice or prescribe the use of any technique as a form of treatment for physical, emotional, or medical problems without the advice of a physician, either directly or indirectly. The intent of the author is only to offer information of a general nature to help you in your quest for emotional and spiritual well-being. In the event you use any of the information in this book for yourself, which is your constitutional right, the author and the publisher assume no responsibility for your actions.

Any people depicted in stock imagery provided by Getty Images are models, and such images are being used for illustrative purposes only. Certain stock imagery © Getty Images.

Print information available on the last page.

ISBN: 978-1-5043-1375-9 (sc)
ISBN: 978-1-5043-1376-6 (e)

Balboa Press rev. date: 07/16/2018

CONTENTS

THE HOOD

L EADERSHIP REQUIRES INDIVIDUALS COMING together for a common purpose. There are many groups that rely on and benefit from each other. These groups are the hoods. Hoods are informal groups and formal organisations that can have the opportunity to bring about synergy and high performances that require coordination and direction. Individuals rely on and operate in several hoods and can have differing roles. These hoods rely on great leadership to exist, thrive, and grow. Leadership has wide-ranging influence and should not be viewed or aspired to as having the opportunity to only be at the top of the chain of command. It needs to be fully realised for the opportunities to bring positive change to hoods (i.e., communities, organisations, academia, neighbourhoods, markets, industries, alliances, teams, and individuals). Regarding such a holistic view to leadership, it should never be taken lightly or for granted. The hoods can be a leader's greatest asset or test, because change is naturally resisted or questioned at the least, and it will always be filled with winners and losers.

The hood is the metaphor to have discussion based on my management and leadership experiences across all the hoods with which I have been involved. This includes both the unpleasant and pleasant aspects of leadership and the impact that comes with the role. Hopefully this starts open and candid discussions on leadership and its requirement for management in all its hoods.

I hope this book will lead to debate and critical thinking regarding the application of leadership as both a guide and stimulus to achieve envisioned

1

outcomes and bring about the high performances that individuals and teams can achieve with direction from leadership and cross collaboration at all levels in the hoods. The leader cannot be successful without having other people to support him or her with management and leadership.

The most crucial point in discussion of the hood is that it is about people and what they can achieve together in collaboration with other hoods.

All the hoods that you are involved with will provide benefits and opportunities for greater performance and self-development. This will provide the positive impact that you can have on people's lives through great leadership, even without being their formal leader.

LEADERSHIP

L EADERSHIP IS A SYSTEM of processes and human arts consisting of creativity, tactics, ideals, and strategic movements. It should not be considered as only being about the control of the hood. The leadership role is to inspire, chart, and determine what the hood needs in all its contexts to improve performance and achieve a continuous evolution towards its vision.

Leadership is having the opportunity to serve, not to be served. This is not to lose sight of the rewards from successful leadership. Leadership is highly sought after for the rewards that are often attached to the position, which can be many things. In many organisations, the leadership role is a reward for previous performances. In some instances, it is even a case of being in the right place at the right time. However, leadership should occur at many levels and in many situations. Once receiving such a role, there is the struggle of remaining the leader through the need to deliver higher performance and have the creativity to develop and provide innovative pathways from which all stakeholders can benefit. There will be suitors for the role within and outside the organisation for the leadership position, and a new leader needs to perform or excite immediately.

Discussing leadership leads discussions on management. Leadership is about the movement and the extracting of higher performances from people, and this will also require professional management practices.

In the management of people and teams for creating change and supporting new leadership, there are issues and conflicts that need to be understood for effective leadership and management. There should also be consideration for the emotional impact it can bring on the leaders and their teams. To have leadership is to bring disruption, and this requires thick skin from the leader to stay the course while initiating change processes and understanding that such disruption brings discontent and, in some cases, militant responses.

Being in charge is not necessarily being the leader. In such cases, leadership direction and actions become situational and create a frequency of review or question as to who the leader is or who is in charge. This can be driven by managers who are the best fit for a given situation to step up or where the leader is preoccupied with other issues and leaves a specific leadership vacuum. This can also be driven by an individual who has political aspirations to lead, and there may be external environmental changes to deal with separately. Often when thinking about leadership, the focus can be on the personal attributes and the characteristics of prominent leaders.

What makes successful leaders? It is more about what they want to do and then do, even though how they do it and whom they do it with is very important. Leading is a progressive action that is about forward change. The substance of strategy and the audacity of the vision of where the leader would like to take the "businesshood" are vital. This leads away from the personal character attributes and more to the aspirational and innovative thinker.

The businesshood is a term I like to use to describe how an organisation is its own neighbourhood. This includes the scope and reach of businesses existing within other hoods and communities and the role that people play to develop and prosper the leader's ideals. A business or organisation and its leader cannot thrive alone. They need to have wide-ranging internal and community support apart from needing to service and interact with other businesses. They also need to satisfy and increase customers, comply with laws and general corporate governance, show environment responsibility, deal with morale issues, and develop their teams in safe, conducive environments. Talking about leadership in the businesshood shows the scope and complexity that is involved, as well as the inherent conflicts and challenges. A greater understanding of the range and scope of leadership responsibilities will show greater appreciation for the rigour of leadership. This will also show that business specialists and executive support teams will appreciate their roles and not underestimate the support that is required and the challenges that leadership must deal with.

As in any neighbourhood, there are diverse groups with wide-ranging views on their own leadership aspirations and with different ideas as to what the vision should be. Then there are those who want the power and the trappings that may come from it, regardless of any wider ramifications. This has been likened to the survival of tribes or subcultures with their own agendas. In acknowledging the differences and the conflicts that are in hoods, we can start to accept that this conflict—or at least tension—exists within the business environments. This presents further challenges for leaders and the different operating environments that exist within organisations.

The challenge for the leader is not to obtain mere consensus but to institute excitement and commitment to executing a strategy, innovating with constant improvement from all learnings and creating an organisational attitude that contains strategies aimed at adding value. This also includes marketing excitedly to customers or constituents on behalf of stakeholders, in both the short term and long term, for sustainable and adaptable growth. I am not saying that a leader should not execute with discipline, but the leader should consider how this discipline is deployed.

There are copious amounts of material and advice on managing performance, and these teach the how-to of management, leadership, and good business practices. The thoughts in the following pages are more on the what and why, along with calling out the chaotic aspects of the leadership environment. This hopefully creates thought on and greater appreciation for what a leader's role is while not taking anything away from great managers and the need for great management. The leader needs to work *on* the business rather than *in* it. It is rare to find a leader who can do both, particularly in the long term.

These thoughts are insights, but I do not proclaim to be an expert. I have been fascinated by leaders and their decisions throughout my career, and although I have not understood them all, they have challenged my thoughts on what is good leadership and why is it necessary. I don't believe that there is a prescription for leadership, but when you come across enduring leadership, it is awesome and something to aspire to, support, demand, and seek.

The most successful leaders that I have witnessed and aspired to learn from have formed a challenging excitement with their teams and have connected with the team members at an individual level. These leaders have always been able to articulate a clear purpose and direction with challenging but manageable objectives. They have always challenged the organisation and its individuals through vision. And they have enabled me to challenge and morph into a leader (to my own surprise) and accept the responsibility, excitement, and honour of developing new leaders.

Development is a keyword throughout the discussion because it is personal development, mentoring, growing, and improving people and teams. This is a wonderful opportunity for the leader to provide further opportunities throughout the hood. Leadership is a movement because there can be no leading without substantial movement from the status quo. I have often been asked, "What is a leader, and how are leaders different from managers?" Through whatever means, leaders provide movement from the status quo, whether they are bringing changes to individuals or developing teams, creating growth, or making major organisational change. In simple terms, they set a course and navigate to the destination with the required resources to reach the objective with new horizons in place before achieving their first objective. They do this with vision and through inspiring and supporting people, often at an individual level.

The hood analogy is meant to create a view on the wide range of influences and executions that impact organisations in today's world. I also like to use the hood apart from its association with a neighbourhood or community to draw on the gang or tribal conflict that exists in the hoods. One must appreciate that leadership and management is not always as pleasant as the textbooks would have one believe. We will look at a fictional business hood shortly, and I hope the analogy gives clarity and provides approaches to your own leadership aspirations with a cool and inspired head.

Leadership is a skilful art requiring the necessary situational skills to guide people to new objectives. Although many would-be leaders have all the certification that enables great managers, they often fall short of leadership aspirations. Leaders need to be savvy and understand that being a leader is not an individual performance role. Leadership encompasses the successful movement of people and their teams, as well as the support and awareness of all internal and external stakeholders. Leadership discussion often centres on the skills that are required rather than the social and emotional skills that I liken to the art of leadership, and it is this talent of having a mix of knowledge and the understanding of people and time that leaders require. Time is a definite factor because leaders and their organisation don't have a lot of it; the leadership tenure is often limited. In moving towards the future vision, which has no defined point as it evolves, so too must the leader and the needs of the organisation evolve. There are leaders who seize this as an opportunity for a revolution, razing the culture, throwing out the old, and even nuking it. However, the savvy leader will inspire and coerce the organisation to evolve, but with their influence and at their speed. Evolution at warp speed requires keeping the foot on the pedal and not losing sight of the need to learn, develop, and obtain timely and latent resources to provide the support and achieve their great vision.

THE BUSINESSHOODS

EVERYTHING APPEARED TO BE normal in the businesshood. The corridors were crowded with the senior managers in deep discussions, trying to stamp their positions in the pecking order of who's who in the hood and lobbying for resources while trying to promote their profile through their very presence. It was just another day typically dominated by managers coping with the ad hoc challenges and reviewing the detailed measurements of the so-called well-managed organisational success. Individual managers are busy staking claims to their own or others' performances regardless of their role and objectives, debating the hood's plans and critiquing their peers; all of this is hopefully for their own benefit. The glitz and show from the spoils of past successes are clear and are the envy of competitor gangs (organisations). The past and current success seems to give credibility and permission for managers to push their own personal agendas and take time away from the vision to consolidate their own position and aspirations. This charade is for personal gain and their own self-interest to remain in power (or to seek more of it). Along with the personal trappings that are on offer, this seems to be seductive, but it's a weakness, threatening the stability and hence the very structural existence of the hood, or at least its continued success. It is breaking down into defensive tactics because it serves its own agendas of being better or the same rather than being great. From what perspective or context is success to be judged, and who is judging it? The current back slapping and patronising views can border on happy talk for what performance is. This type of group self-assessment can be further manifested by group think and self-interest. There is no leadership because the leader is beholden to so many managers with differing demands, misleading the leader (whether purposely or not) and causing everyone to lose sight of the vision. The leader's behaviour is modified by the groupthink reinforcements and is lost in the bureaucratic requirements and demands for the daily operational, compliance demands, internal and external stakeholders, and competitive forces influencing its execution of strategy and subsequent performance. This is more in line with developing or managing propaganda programs than real strategic, vision-led management, but this activity has everyone feeling comfortable and engaged.

Without inspired leadership, there is only management. The leader is merely managing court each day, surveying the vista of smiling, chatting individuals who are the representatives of their teams and charged with the responsibility of delivering the programs and results, as well as managing their continued existence. They are almost crying out for defined leadership. The teams of people have formed their own tribes with their symbols, micro strategies, and their own propaganda, jargon, and symbols that are a code to those in the know of which sub tribal gang they belong, aspire to, or are beholden to. Posters start to go up on walls, new key performance targets emerge (and there are heaps of them), and discussions in hallways are typical of a political process for the further breakdown of leadership and performance. All this activity is to further reinforce their propaganda for self-benefit in pushing their own positions or to undermine peers or their leader while appearing to be very busy.

It's obvious that there is something untoward happening akin to political disorganisation and with reactive alliances forming based on the situation at hand. These alliances are based on self-promotion and personal gain, or fear of being alone and being outside the sphere of power and security. The leader is inept or certainly out of his depth in allowing the disparate behaviours to continue, although they are disguised by the over-the-top supportive commentary to the leader. This leads to the question of whether there can be successful strategy or performance without great leadership. This is where a plan and strategy separate in definition.

Where are the management teams, the group values, and the subsequent behaviours that are meant to be the very substance for the organisation's performance and integrity? The very structure of the hood is marching to an informal beat that is unpredictable and extremely chaotic in situational responses and sudden changes, rather than being directed by an overarching, strategic vision. The rush of sudden tactical changes, often driven by the so-called need for stabilising the organisation, manifests with its unpredictable behaviour into almost a metaphor for its being in control. Examples of this in the hood are obvious character assassinations, backstabbing, liars, sabotage, overlooking of talent, political advantage, petty theft of time, lack of transparency, short-term reporting of goals, preventable accidents, meetings for the sake of meetings, almost daily changes in direction, and capitulation to the market by reacting only to the competition. But most of all, there is a lack of innovation and discipline.

There is constant justification of management performances with pitches and presentations that all is well. In all this confusion, the leader is led into the predicament of justifying their own position. The accountants or scorers of performance are asked to be creative and provide greater detail, which will ultimately lead to a situation of no further creative exercise other than to save the day. Any new direction is sought to continue the organisation's success through its so-called stabilisation or marking of time. Leadership is required to keep the strategy organic and pertinent to achieving the vision.

This results in a seemingly nice but underground hostile environment which could be compared to the most organised and structured business team environments, such as one would imagine being in the highest profile of organisations. The businesshood can be a brutal and a somewhat chaotic group of teams. What is the remedy to a facade of such a dynamic but reactive organisation, and what can be done?

The police (the human resources and operational teams) are absent because the tribes control the culture and apply the rules, and it is lawless to the organisation's vision and constitution. How could an organisation operating in such a valueless, self-serving culture be successful, and is the success the fuel to such ad hoc and self-interest behaviours?

The obvious question is, Where's the organisations leadership?

We enter the discussion and exploration into leadership in business and its challenges with the façade stripped away. Hopefully this picture leads us in to a more real discussion on leadership rather than a purist's direction and focus on contemporary management practices. I am no academic and admire those who are, but too often we only have a discussion on management roles and leadership from the academic view rather than from the practical side. Hopefully this creates further discussion and outcomes.

By observation, the answer is simple. It is typical of many non-performing has-been organisations that are hanging on to current or past glories with vision past and gone. Survival is the goal, with little leadership other than short-term, gang-like domination for its functional survival. There is plenty of resource and skill that has internalised itself on the hood. What has happened outside of the hood? Who is looking over the fence to review what is happening in the external environment? Who is considering the future to provide direction and a unifying vision for the hood in order to form a high-performance community? Leadership requires risk and insight on so many platforms.

It is apparent that disciplined strategic leadership is missing even though the management processes in the hood are environmentally perceived as best, specialists prevail, and there are designated functional leaders that have the responsibility to lead the hood to become a high-performance community. It is going to require overarching, long-termed vision based orientated leadership. In simple terms, there is no single direction or point to reach (i.e., vision). What is leadership, how is it to be applied, and how does it make a difference? How is the leader measured? Effective leadership is not a popularity contest. Remember that the hood is in soft anarchy: it will require definite, consistent, and compelling leadership, with consequences for unaligned behaviours. The hood is energetic and talented, but its weakness can be its past success as it continually tries to reinvent itself in its past successful form or drift off into sub-strategic tangents. Leadership is a risky change process that can only move forward, and without any strategic aligned change program, leadership will not be effective or even exist. Although it may be said to be in place, it's only being managed to temporarily bring the gangs together as a dictator would—until another gang member seizes the opportunity to overthrow and commences the same dictatorial, leaderless cycle again. Beware of this developing culture in an organisation, poor leaders tend to develop poor leaders. This is a travesty in loss of experienced talent within the organisation or what could be brought in.

In reviewing the hood, we need to understand why it exists. The hood and its stakeholders should be beneficiaries of their leader's purpose and objectives, and they serve those who enable success (sometimes called its customers), whether internal or external.

The gangs must transform into supportive collaborative teams, and leadership needs to become a driving, supportive, guiding force based on the hood's agreed values and goals. One must develop the culture instituted by the leader's vision of what could be. Leadership is much more than the style of a person; it is about spirit and vision. It is what could be accomplished with a plan on how it could be so.

As the hood expands with geographic reach, market share, and competency, the leadership needs to grow from theory-based, top-down direction to direct support based on a high vision strategy and systemised management. The right team (gang) needs to empower the leader through its support, be confident in providing innovative feedback, accept organisational leadership, and be leaders of their own teams in delivering high performance.

Let's discuss the strategies of establishing leadership in such a hostile environment. First, we need to address the denial that all is fine in the hood today, as all the smiling faces acknowledge and greet each other while they prepare to survive another day in driving the hood's performance.

The hood is hopefully an apt metaphor, suggesting that organisations are not simple and not always nice. They are compiled of teams that should be working in a complete synchronicity and direction with harmony, for the benefit of all stakeholders. Serving and satisfying customers with the right strategy and sub-strategies should see all stakeholders as beneficiaries.

Why the hood? It will hopefully create a discussion through acknowledging the abstract and wide range of people relationships and their roles that challenge the silent compliance and disengagement that tends to accompany the pretence of many organisations that are said to be aligned. Contribution is evident, but is it consistent and constant with the strategy as to what is needed (synchronicity) and the two Cs, consistency and constancy, of effort requiring every contribution to add value and bring movement that is strategised to satisfy and benefit all strategic stakeholders. What type of character is required to belong and then lead in the hood? This is an important question and requires observation because character and subsequent behaviour is critical. Not what is said, but what is done inspires the hood or organisation to mimic and develop aligned behaviours, which may or may not be conducive to the strategy and its goals. Standards are set by policy and implemented through behaviours, with leadership being the prime example.

Stepping out of the typical organisational analysis hopefully provides both an objective review of the current organisation and innovative thought on what it needs and could be. Reviewing and discussing leadership from different and various angles shows the wide-ranging impact and reach that leaders and their leadership have on hoods.

This abstract view or analysis can create a new context for establishing the environment reality rather than what a strategy paper purports to do, reviewing and implementing operational behaviours within systems and enabling the team performance to be understood before impacting on the culture and its systems for delivering performance

In selection to the hood, a person and his or her response to the hood's environment should have them considered with a contribution expectation at 100 per cent and their likely category fit and team fit to the hood's culture. They can then be scored from the high expectation, marking them down based on any inability to adapt for continued contribution to the strategy. This can highlight developmental needs or replacement for high performance to be maintained and increase growth. There needs to be some measurement to understand direction and movement because leadership needs to bring forward-based change for there to have been leadership. This maintains the expectation of 100 per cent performance. Note that expectation increases, as does the vision, with progress.

In developing the discussion on leadership, we need to measure direction towards the vision and the application of strategy, ensuring that the strategy is a feasible one.

The operating culture is becoming more complex as the environment becomes more difficult, with the external forces and internal business rules for so-called transparency and legislative compliance. The emphasis is on organisational development and performance—in short, striving to make people within the team better, rather than making the operating environment easier for people to contribute and excel. The adage of "keep it simple" never goes away.

The ground forces are bound to further struggle without leadership binding the specialities and characters of middle management to the strategic goals of obtaining the vision and managing the operating environment. This has all been discussed so far without mentioning the objective for this entire chaos, which is satisfying customers that deal with the hood.

Empowerment within the boundaries of strategy and operating within lawful policies should not be an abdication of leadership but a precursor to innovation as the leader stewards the vision and distributes resource, control, and support applicable to the operating environment and market demands (i.e., external demands and forces). Empowerment of the teams requires great trust and an understanding to the teams, because operating under empowerment is difficult without the right direction and support from the leader.

Now that we have an abstract platform for consideration, enabling a stepping out of the current organisational environment, we can review the specific requirements and trials of leadership and management. The issue is how to coordinate and lead a team of specialists, which is a requirement of the modern business and education system that turns out specialists with narrow views rather than the understanding of contributing and collaborating in businesseshoods that operate in very diverse, dynamic markets and environments. It is to be expected that with these different schools of thought and application, there is conflict.

Managers have a strong role because achievement of their team objectives at all costs will exacerbate the dysfunction within the hood and foster clandestine teams that put on happy faces without addressing the issues that will effectively damage the more holistic performance and distribution of benefits. This may imply a position that leaders command too much attention and reward over their key management teams, rather than focusing on all the roles. Focus can be placed on the reward rather than winning the vision.

The point of the hood is that organisations need to be so much more than surviving entities. They are a community that relies on the leadership of their leaders, who have the way for development and the ultimate handing over of leadership with a legacy of a visionary platform from which to continue working. This is what separates great organisations from the anarchy analogy of the hood.

There are many types of leadership, and they have been categorised, described, and named by many. Every organisation has its own descriptors and names of various leadership and management styles that it has experienced or is currently experiencing, whether they are negative or positive. The point is that leadership comes with review and critique, driven by many objectives and judged by many.

One type of leadership style is the self-publicist, who tends to lead successful organisations and is seen from the outside to be the prime reason for it. This type of self-promotion can be very subtle and is propagated from not giving public credit to the individuals and teams that are more the reason for the success. The self-publicist leader benefits from that success.

The worst part of this is that he tends to pass the baton to other self-publicist leaders, who again keep a lid on those who really deserve the credit and benefit from their efforts. This quiet self-promotion is recognised by the teams in the organisation and can be divisive and frustrating. These types of leaders rarely have a far-reaching organisational vision, instead providing a short-term vision for their own self-promotion and or self-benefit. The issue here is that for the high-performance managers to be recognised and receive the appropriate rewards leave, and as a result they may join the opposition.

There has been much stated about categorising leaders and managers into types and styles through studies and observations. I will leave that to those who wish to try to take such a scientific approach to the quirks of human behaviour. I would like to discuss another group that I call the spectators. Spectators are those who commentate and give opinions on what should or should not have happened without having played on the field. This type of commentating is usually negative and aimed at bringing down those leaders and managers who embrace innovation and are willing to determine what is for the betterment of the organisation as they make decisions and execute them. Although spectators will often publicly agree with the leader to remain in favour, this can have a cascading effect in groupthink by other managers behaving similarly, with the result that the organisation is driven only by the leader receiving patronising feedback. Remember the story of the emperor and his new clothes. As the leader, you can have a person who does not take kindly to any difference of opinion and easily takes umbrage in debate. Like the emperor, allowing this type of support will be to the leader's detriment—and consequently the organisation's. There are savvy subordinates who will use such patronising support of their leaders to bring them down and open an opportunity for themselves. Political behaviour has so many disguises and purposes, but it is usually distilled down to self-interest. The outcome can be the same disaster from groupthink, with the leader being the patsy rather than the coach.

Spectators like to get close to the coach (leader) and influence through their opinions, which more often than not are self-serving and politically motivated rather than reflections from which everyone can benefit. Alas, you can apply the eighty-twenty rules, where 20 per cent of the organisation gets 80 per cent of the objectives. I guess that leaves 80 per cent in the grandstand at some time, which questions the efficiency of such a latent resource.

That's enough about categorising. Let's talk about the aspects that we can apply ourselves as leaders and the issues that need to be dealt with.

The hood is organic and cannot be controlled by self-interest because every individual and team has control of his or her own destiny. It is a question for leadership as to what type of destiny and environment leaders are offering to their teams. Every individual should be a beneficiary from great leadership, guidance, and resources. There is no prescription for great leadership. Rather, great visionaries are needed who can inspire and deliver a greatness and purpose to the people who make up the organisation.

I believe future leaders will be generalists who can understand and support a range of senior managers with their specialised skills and understand where and when they will be best used to achieve the organisation's strategic ambitions. These rare leaders do not necessarily come about from academia but are avid learners through the academic system, from experience, or both. They are examples of other successful managers and leaders. This is typical of those who have the intelligence to learn and are high in emotional intelligence, having the ability to understand fellow humans and support their well-being and development while also self-benefiting from their interactions. They have open minds and a keen radar for learning and embracing continuous improvement. These types of leaders and managers operate above their own self-interests and lead by putting others first, either individually or as the organisation. They will usually benefit through the results themselves because of their team's achievements. This type of leadership takes courage and personal vision, as well as belief in the organisation's vision and their role being one of high contribution. These types of leaders believe in people. Be wary of fearful leaders who will surround themselves with scapegoats and teams of specialists for self-protection rather than the organisation's benefit—and worse still, increasing waste and costs. These types are usually identified through high turnover rates of their direct reports.

Let's move through many of the key issues and views that I have formed through my own interests and experiences. I will share my views, although I am unable to be directive. This is the key to my messages, because the hood is dynamic and decision making will be bound by constraints, context, and opportunity that make leadership such a wonderful role for those who enjoy people, innovation, excitement, growth, and satisfaction from leading and developing others for what has not been done before. Remember that there will be a need for future leaders to carry on your excellent work.

THE VISION

WHAT IS A VISION, and how do you get it? A vision preamble is a meaningful description of aspirations for all aspects of the organisation. It can inspire and satisfy the relevant stakeholders with the descriptive of what the performance and culture of the organisation should look like and become. The vision is a brief blueprint into the envisioned future with a creative understanding of what inspires innovation. It provides the direction along with the designated attitudes for fostering change and what the organisation needs to be. Having a descriptive brief is paramount for a dynamic and all-encompassing vision. The vision has its own inclusive goals, which are to reward the contributors and beneficiaries for its achievement while describing the type of culture, interpersonal relationships, and standards for the hood to become a high-performance organisation. It also addresses where its sits in the external frameworks of markets and communities (i.e., the hoods).

With visions being openly communicated in varied media, it can be easy to forget who they are intended for and why. They need to be heard, understood, and inspiring to all who have a contributing role. A well-articulated vision needs to also have merit with external stakeholders in seeing the organisation as one of merit with which they would like to align. Marketing departments can have a specialist role to support the leader in articulating and communicating the vision. The vision needs to span and inspire beneficial change for all, with the contributing efforts and behaviour expectations of the envisioned businesshood.

The vision is not just a fantastic thought bubble that the leader has brought forward. It needs to be a considered vision for the operating areas, opportunities, resources, and competencies that make its achievement rewarding and viable.

The hood (organisation) needs to understand where it is heading and why, and how the gang (team) benefits. The senior executive team (specialists) with their own organisation and resources need to understand and be totally committed before detailing their sub-strategies for specialised focus within their own teams in contributing to the master strategy as well as their own specific accountabilities. These specialised teams need to perform while understanding their fit within the strategy and how their efforts are value adding with the performance of the other teams that have separate groups and are accountable as the one team (i.e., the organisation's performance) for which the leader is responsible.

In keeping the master vision simple, it should only deal with the high-level objectives and not encroach on detailing to the sub-strategies that should be empowered to the executive teams to lead and manage. The vision should detail where the organisation is going. The strategy will detail the way it will get there and spell out the values and benefits to be shared by all stakeholders. It will also detail the type of organisation that it would like to be viewed as and what is considered successful performance.

The vision can be a simple document but needs to have the organisation stretch and grow even if it falls short of the vision objective. Visions can be very comprehensive and descriptive depending on the degree of change and the actual vision. A great vision will be rejected initially, or at least viewed by many with trepidation and scepticism, because it should be audacious enough to drive new thoughts, behaviours, and innovation, which are to be embedded into a new strategic blueprint. A vision is doomed to failure without a strategy.

In preparing the vision, the leader should engage the organisation at all levels and address its deficiencies and opportunities. In selling the vision, the leader needs to articulate why it is necessary for the organisation and where there are rewards and benefits for all stakeholders. These should be on all levels: intrinsic, extrinsic, social, and community. For the leader's and the vision's creditability, these need to be presented as doable, realistic, and truthful, including a plan.

Aim for the stars, and if you hit the moon, it may not be too bad a shot. If you miss, work out why and give it another shot. Revise the vision statement and its subsequent strategy.

The vision statement should be concise and inspirational, setting which type of stars you would like to hit, rather than a detailed vision giving a more guided view of how the leader would like to see the organisation be, by when, and for what purpose. This is a précis, statement, or snapshot of the vision.

Some could see it as unreachable and uncomfortable, but it needs to be strong enough to force game-changing thinking and strong fellowship. Forget about the detail in the statement and focus on the inspiration and the opportunity for unleashing talent to achieve exciting change and new goals.

MISSION STATEMENT

T HE MISSION STATEMENT IS a very concise explanation of the purpose of the organisation. Why do they exist and for what purpose, and who and how do they do it with, and to whom? Note that it is not defined regarding when and how much. This statement is meant to help stay the course and aid operating (management), direction, and communication to all stakeholders. The mission needs to be clear and nonspecific in its goal-orientated aspirations, but it should not be too abstract because that leads to a lot more imagination and hence interpretation.

Mission statements are normally open to all, and as in the case of communication, the intended audience needs to be considered. Receipt, acceptance, and understanding of the message should be monitored.

VALUES

ARTICULATING A VISION AND formulating its strategy is one thing, but guidelines for internal and external operational cooperation and collaboration need to be agreed as a precursor for the most appropriate behaviours to reach high performance and complete the vision.

Stating and managing to both the organisational and personal values is so much more than the obvious because it gives a licence for the individuals and teams to develop the culture via the vast diversity that exists within teams and hoods. People will have individual and personal values which may be very different, but it is not acceptable for these to drive behaviours that are outside that of the hood's agreed and acceptable behaviours. With the correct motivational programs, the adherence to the hood's values will set up the right behavioural changes that bring about a high-performing culture, which is conducive to the execution of the strategy and is beneficial to all stakeholders.

A new leader should approach an organisation by having to address the values as a matter of urgency in order to gain insights of its current culture, how the strategy will be activated, and people being able to behave within the agreed values and understand the reasons for the ones that require change. There is much more to be said in having agreed values in place.

STRATEGY

WHAT IS STRATEGY COMPARED to a plan? There are many approaches that can be taken in addressing any issue, and I liken plans and strategy to process and systems. Plans are the subsets of a strategy, and processes are the subsets that make up systems. The strategy is the aggregate of plans that create the overarching and far-reaching strategy, which considers the synergistic activities of all the teams and contributing stakeholders. The strategy may have a longer timeline than most plans. Strategy is the all-encompassing sum of the detailed plans for the mobilisation and achievement of the organisation's vision. It gives primary direction, resource, permission, and expectations to achieve the vision, charting the course to follow.

The biggest challenge is not devising strategy but activating the strategy while remaining focused on achieving the vision and at the same time maintaining the flexibility to adapt. The leader is responsible for every aspect of the strategy, including the performance of the organisation, keeping it fit to purpose and on track.

All-encompassing means that each executive arm or division has a detailed, specific plan of its expected contribution to the vision regarding who, where, what, and when, with a score sheet with personal responsibilities to ensure that there is accountability at the individual and team levels. Also, they must understand and appreciate that theirs is but one piece of the puzzle; the goal is to have all pieces come together to form the strategic picture in synchronicity.

In being strategic, it should also itemise the issues, timings, and internal conflicts that may impede progress or external issues or regulations that require discussion, resource, or support.

Strategic leadership is engaging and requires the development and implementation of the executive team to have the support and resources to deliver on their accountabilities for their functional strategy. That they are implementing processes that are cross-complementing to others, and an executive team is then focussed on the strategic vision.

Every output, whether it is simple communication, process, or involvement with external stakeholders, needs to be synchronised towards achieving the vision. Politics and internal peer review will be the biggest threat. All other threats are normally transparent, and the political threats are not so easy to see and recognise. Do not overlook these threats to a successful strategy.

Strategy is the very challenge of leadership for developing it and then executing it. When speaking about leadership, you cannot move too far away from strategy because it is the action to achieve the vision. A strategy without leadership becomes nothing more than a plan; hence, a strategy is very actionable.

Leadership in developing strategy should not use its power to create a revolution, but to allow resourced evolution. This puts an emphasis on improving the businesshood's environment, and individuals can improve and grow at a faster pace than ever before; certainly it's faster than the competition.

The leader's role in strategy is detailing and enacting a plan for productive change, providing guidance by constructive movement towards the vision. It is the leader's role to decide on any deviation or change in the strategy. This process is paradoxically creating the biggest challenge for the leader to remain the leader (in position and behaviourally) while being constructive, supportive, politically savvy, and cohesive in driving change and producing satisfactory results. The leader must also remain on the pathway to the vision that is organically changing because of its progress (or lack thereof) via its own changing dynamics. This is where a clearly articulated strategy navigating towards the vision supports the structure and goals of the leadership's regime. Progress needs to be continually checked, and strategic execution should be adapted within the capability of the organisation. Therefore, leadership is about creating feasible strategy, and there can be no successful leadership without a plausible strategy. How do we measure leadership if there is no strategic means to achieve great vision and keep it accountable? This brings in the argument that leadership is much more than positional power.

Leadership has destiny, and the destination needs to be defined and plotted. Leaders are often in the unenviable position of having to say no, but you don't have a strategy if you never say no.

There is always the question as to what strategy is and therefore what leadership is. To me, leadership is not about who you are but what you can move an organisation towards. There can be no greater accolade than developing individuals and teams to greater performance, seeing them enjoying the benefits that are derived from such performance.

Strategy can be very detailed but should not be overcomplicated. As with communication, direction needs to be believable, doable, and understandable. Keep it simple and give clear definition to instructions. Have a means for frequent feedback on performance. As with all changing environments, it requires attitude to embrace change and accept that strategy will be required to change. A well-led movement dictates this necessity.

In devising strategy, you need to work on the strategic environment, as well as define goals in keeping it simple for teams to manage. Make it easier for people to be great rather than wishing and driving them to greatness (or failure through) complicated operating environments. A smart leader will develop strategy and provide resources that enable successful strategy execution through a simplified operating environment.

Strategy is often used as a buzzword for actions that are not to be argued against. Strategy needs to have substance that is embedded with policy and processes supported by information. It also needs committed team members with continuous improvement attitudes that allow strategy to evolve as the operating and external environments evolve and change. This does not mean that strategy cannot be questioned. It should be continually scrutinised to ensure that the course is resourced and is set to the vision.

GOALS AND MILESTONES

F YOU HAVE A huge problem, the easiest way to solve it is to break it down into manageable, achievable pieces. To achieve a great vision is to see it as a set of jigsaw pieces of set goals. It is much the same principle of breaking the strategy into goals and milestones and delegating the actions for their achievement to the best individuals, teams, or other management programs to ensure that the goals are reached (i.e., project teams, cross-functional teams, or third-party resources). The leader is deconstructing the vision into jigsaw pieces, with roles assigned to their development. Then with the reality of managing the vision pieces into operating pieces, there is collaboration with all the other pieces to create a completed timely, working strategy to achieve the vision.

Creating such a stairway system requires each step to be set a target with responsibilities that lead to the next target step, and so on. Setting milestones and timings with accountability is accounted for in the strategy.

Although the vision can seem a long way off for its realisation, creating pathways and goals that are very pertinent and achievable can bring on belief and create a life and energy for the strategy to be successfully achieved one step at a time. Synchronicity of individuals and teams can allow for multiple steps to be simultaneously achieved.

MANAGEMENT EXECUTION

TYPICALLY, WHEN DISCUSSING MANAGEMENT, control becomes a keyword that is bandied about, but this is somewhat counter intuitive when senior managers are about a specific role or it should be said leading strategic programs and teams. This can be the point where the strategic vision breaks down and subcultures develop. Although effort is towards the execution of strategy, management without leadership application will not achieve the strategy. This goes against the whole argument of discussing leadership and management separately, because they both require management and leadership disciplines, particularly management with its specialised skills. Leadership skills are required to manage teams of individuals to achieve the strategy. Measurement is a prime tool used by managers. Too few measures can fracture an organisation, and too many can confuse or, due to their complication, become ignored. Combating this requires the division of all the measures communicated to the relevant teams. Measures can be divisive and inconsistent to bringing about common operating themes and a collaborating culture that would be consistent with the strategic vision if they are not aligned, relevant, and accountable. Senior management are very skilful and have driven teams that have many functional team purposes. There needs to be an understanding of how and why these purposes react to make the organisation successful, and that one team's success along with another's means that they both did well because they both contributed to the organisations performance. This is the leader's predicament in aligning team performance to strategic performance.

The success of management teams in a synchronistic way brings about successful performance that is often taken for granted because "it just happens", so to speak. Leaders should not overlook this synchronistic outcome because it can have a harmonious outcome over the various management teams providing that they are recognised for their individual contributing performance. Such harmony and acknowledgement as to the benefits of synchronistic outcomes increase the capacity and collaboration amongst the teams.

Execution on strategy requires teams that are led by very skilful managers who are on-board with the leader's vision, and it is rare to find those who can fiercely operate in the moment and still find the time to creatively think about what can be. Maybe the best leaders are great managers who have a dream or the capacity to do so.

Managers are often outcomes of academia, and this can have them model-driven and looking for history to provide solutions and to measure success. They will be stretched to reach their high-level strategic outcomes, and they will need to have the attributes of not just performing well but also being innovative and creative, or else they will find conflict with the visionary goals of the leader. The leader has a role to develop these highly skilled managers into leader-driven managers

Therefore, the leader needs to give these groups of managers his time to constantly brief them on the progress of the organisation to its vision so that there is holistic ownership of the organisation's results, as well as for what they are each responsible. The leader needs to trust the managers to execute without overlooking non-performance. He must continually keep the mindset of the implementers of strategy in tune with the vision. Leadership takes courage and resilience. It can be viewed as a tough business, but with the vision's course set, the majority will always benefit and therefore seek to contribute.

Leaders are usually very highly rewarded, and I think that there is too great a disparity between their recognition and reward and that of the key senior managers who implement all the pieces of the strategic jigsaw with both intrinsic and extrinsic benefits.

I believe there is an emerging paradigm for leadership teams, and future discussion will be on the development and compensation of these teams rather than such a singular focus on the prime leader. This will change traditional leadership and senior management behaviours and organisational structure, with a blending of high performance and high skill sets to lead organisations. This will be a challenge for boards that are normally conservative but are having wider governance issues to deal with overseeing the business performance and the interests of shareholders. This by no means diminishes the importance of leadership; it sees it as being more dynamic and team based. If the organisational structure of boards works, why wouldn't a similar approach to executive management teams, with the leader behaving more like a chairman and coach but with overall authority, vision, and accountability? The emphasis is to have leadership at the head of cultural development.

The issue for leaders is that as businesses grow and become more complex and global, the skill sets required are greater and wider, along with cultural and legislative differences. This will require very competent, committed, diverse senior management teams to lead the strategy.

I think that it is fair to say that you can overly manage but not overly lead.

ENVIRONMENTAL LEADERSHIP

INTERNAL ISSUES

1. Operations

THE LEADER AND THE executive team will have the greatest influence on the success, rate of change, and alignment of the culture to the organisation's vision. The ability to secure adequate resources can be a benefit or handbrake on the team's and the overall organisation's progress. The leader sets the tone and attitude for the organisations motivation and behaviours, as well as the allocation of resources. At times, it will be necessary for her to be an evangelist, teacher, judge, jury, and executioner. There may be times that you need to let the most competent executive go, but setting the culture requires consistency in decision-making and setting examples that reflect the culture as envisioned. A worthwhile saying to keep in mind is, "What you allow is what you teach." Again, leadership is about what you do and with whom rather than what you say. In leadership judgement, there will always be reflection and categorisation (or grouping) by those who review leadership performance or study it for development and learning purposes.

What is style? It is the sum of the leader's personal culture: voice, grooming expertise, storytelling, communication, skills, passion, demeanour, ability to deal with stress, truth telling, and history. I will let you add to these examples, but it is all those attributes, as well as past and expected performance, that make up the leader's character. Apart from having a reasonable IQ, there will need to be a very high level of emotional intelligence and social intelligence (i.e., understanding individuals and groups). Leaders need to have a thick skin because there will be unpopular questioning and change resistance, but this goes with the territory. Leaders need to exhibit trust, but this needs to be tempered with a healthy scepticism and curiosity for the pertinent facts for the journey towards the vision. Operation is about execution and performance, and there can be digressions (implied or not) imbedded in operational management strategy.

Senior managers need to have all the leadership skills but are tasked with specific performance targets. They will need to have talent and organisational skills in managing teams to achieve the strategy. The problem for senior managers is that they are normally reviewed and rewarded on performance alone. This may be of benefit to the organisations success, but it's problematic for the leader in progressing the culture and remaining on track towards the future vision. When there are managers who are promoted to leadership positions based solely on their high performance, they may not be able to bring the required leadership behaviours. Such a discipline achieves objectives at an all-costs approach with the wider responsibilities of a senior leadership position. This is not a shortcoming of the senior manager but of the leader, who should identify these leadership candidates early and establish leadership development programs for them. The human resource team should play a significant role with the leader in providing a personnel development and succession strategy, as well as programs for seamless transition and human resource depth for any management changes. With a performance-only agenda, an organisation will be reduced to scrambling with the other incumbent issues for which it has responsibility.

The issue for the senior manager and all who aspire for leadership within their current or future organisations is to have an awareness that the current accolades that they may be receiving may not be the criteria for shortlisting to the interview stage for more senior leadership selection. I have seen a lot of managers address this through politicking, to the detriment of the organisation. I suggest that the manager seeking leadership include self-critiquing as a positive aspect of the personality— not for self-destructive purposes but for analysing the areas required for one's own personal development and learning. The other recommendation is to network and become involved with positive self-promotion within and without the organisation, and to help and support others at every opportunity because this will promote and develop one's personal brand. Remember that there is the human condition for obligation (or call it karma or paying back). The best type of self-promotion comes from others supporting your aspirations, and most leadership candidates are nominated for leadership roles by their peers and outside stakeholders. If the current leader has a self-appointed heir, it will be very difficult to circumvent the inevitable and, keeping this in mind, shape one's own leadership and career aspirations.

Leaders like to have a close association with their senior management teams, and although this can be quite fruitful for the teams during times of successful performance when the leader leaves, there can be a lot of collateral damage. If a manager has not been managing his own personal brand, he will suffer the same exit fate as the leader—without the benefits. This is not saying that they should not closely support the leader, because if the leader fails, it will also be failings in the senior management group. This highlights the need to manage your own brand, and the leader's team will be categorised as being much the same as the leader. Therefore, it is in the senior management team's interest to support and enhance the brand of the leader, their team, and the organisation. It is very important to not fall into a myopic existence that all their worth and benefit only exists within the one organisation. The power of external networking with other beneficiaries of the organisation, and within the community with likeminded associations, can be very handy for personal growth and an escape route if ever needed when overlooked for one's career aspirations. It is very easy to become absorbed in the one organisation, and this can have a myopic effect on one's leadership aspirations.

There are recognised leadership positions, and these are well rewarded and strived for, but there is a requirement for leadership at all levels of an organisation and should exist at every human interaction and endeavour. In my experience, a promotion is given to those who already demonstrate capability and leadership. Leadership positions are not given on academic merit but the ability to have demonstrated the support, capability, capacity, and the leadership style that fits with a role, its team, and the organisation to enable its ongoing progress towards the vision. In short, you get a role if you have already been doing it in the eyes of the reviewers, and you are likely to have organisational support.

Operating the business leadership is paramount, but because operations has been deemed to be the mantle of the experienced manager driven on performance, there can be conflict with other senior supporting roles creating organisational complexity. This has been countered by the creation of more senior roles, resulting in further conflict by overmanaging rather than leading (i.e., divisional general managers and chief operating titles trying to manage this division through title rather than leadership, supporting all functions appropriately).

2. Resources

Managers continually lobby the leader and seek favour for a greater share of resources and favour in order to achieve more for their own influence. In some cases, this is for personal gain and advancement in the organisation, or to disadvantage another department or manager, rather than what is best overall.

A lot more is given to the theory and discussion of scarce resources, and an efficient and vibrant organisation should always be in a state of scarce resource as it is advancing to its vision at speed.

I have been in very difficult situations where senior managers have been lobbying for resources and actions that are very much needed but are outside the current level of capability and capacity of the organisation. This type of narrow-mindedness is about a manager's single view on her own department needs without appreciating or understanding the organisation's whole position and what is in keeping with the strategy. In my case, the leader allowed this persistent lobbying and conflict to continue, creating pressure to reapply resources and project timelines. This type of conflict does not find its own natural level or solution. It was very evident, in what I experienced, that the department managers in these cases where not willing to step back and learn that there was a wider strategic issue other than what they had put into their own plan or using the position for increasing their own exposure with the leader. These managers were more interested in pushing their own agenda rather than understanding that it was outside the current strategic timing and available resource. This is where a genuine leader can support and develop managers without sacrificing progress to the vision within the hood's capacity. This type of behaviour cascades into personal politicking and divisive teams.

Although difficult at times, it is the leader's mantle to allocate and direct resources and actions with the overarching understanding of the strategic position and direction of the organisation. Egos are often bruised in these situations, but that goes with senior management roles and leadership

3. Tenure

Time is the key criteria in managing a leader's tenure because it will be a strategic piece of time in the organisation's life, which has a purpose and a basis for an ultimate handover to achieve the continuing evolution of the vision and the organisation's growth. It is a sobering thought and a great motivator to get things done as prudently and quickly as possible for all the leaders to have a differing leadership style and skills, which are needed for the advancement through the stages of the organisation's growth and the environments in which it operates. A successful leader will ultimately lead himself to his own end in that role. Hopefully he has a strategy for where he goes next.

4. Succession

After discussing tenure, it leads to succession and whether the leader wants to be directly involved in the handover process. Succession development is one of the nicest and most difficult roles for the leader. A common mistake that I have often witnessed was leaders and senior managers replacing themselves with a likeness, or someone they would have liked to be or imagined they were. Although this may be self-gratifying, it may not be best for the organisation. This is a challenge that a mature and vision-based leader will have little trouble with, because the focus is on the business evolution and its seamless handover. From day one of a leader's role, he should be thinking about his replacement and developing likely candidates. A replacement can be sourced from within or outside of the organisation; this will be based on the organisation's current situation and the situation for the leader's departure.

The successor will have her own style and aspirations, but with the right succession strategy, she should be well versed in the organisation's capacity and issues. Her first one hundred days should be very dynamic and capture the trust of the organisation. The organisation should expect more from the new leader because she has a freshness and enthusiasm to stamp her presence and style on her teams and all the stakeholders.

This leads to a new discussion on candidate selection, and the leader needs to understand that once the new leader is in place, there may be a new or revised approach to the vision. This is the way of the world, and it's why organisations prosper and fail due to how leaders lead. It may be difficult to accept, but a new leader should consider if there is any mentoring opportunity from the previous leader. At the least, he should consider council from the senior team without relinquishing their authority to make their own decisions. A leader cannot abdicate from their accountability.

5. Capability

Leaders can destroy an organisation, or his own personal standing, through getting too far ahead of an organisation's capability in implementing its strategy. Older schools of thought managed this by conducting pilot programs and staggered roll-outs of the latest programs. Today's world moves much faster than that, and if the change program is devised to bring about competitive advantage, then it needs to move faster because competitors can emulate or overtake a program through learning or emulating from yours.

Leaders need to have an appreciation of the organisation's capability in its intelligence and emotional capacity to achieve its strategic plan and resource it accordingly with contingency and escape plans.

It is fair to say that most teams will underestimate their capability and capacity to achieve, but if the leader has a keen insight and instituted a learning organisation, it will find its feet quickly and innovate to greater heights. Morale, belief, and trust must be embedded in the culture through the leader's leadership for the teams to stretch to new levels.

How do you know if you can run a marathon without running one? It takes belief and courage to give it a go and stepping out of one's comfort zone. Organisations can become very institutionalised and staid. Programs need to be put into place to break out of this. This can be achieved simply by having a social get-together and themed and tactful, fancy dress days to break down social barriers. If this can involve customers and other stakeholders, even better. This is, all to have greater acceptance of change and what is different, with individuals feeling comfortable to express themselves in group situations.

6. Capacity

Obviously, there is a need for capability in terms of skill set for the role, but the human strength of diverse teams with great organisational fit will have surprising capacity as the need arises. The leader has a paramount role in setting the scene for this to take place.

A champion team will beat a team of champions. This occurs so often in the sporting arena, and organisations are no different. Improving capacity in the human and technical environment is clear to most, but having the strategy that fits the skill and drive of the organisation while having programs in place that improve capacity is the key to gaining strategic efficiency.

It is often the goal of an organisation to have a high-performance team, but leaders should also look to create high-capacity teams. The key trait should be their adaptability and demeanour to adapt to fast change even if it can appear to be a U-turn or a complete change in strategy. Managers who are multiskilled or mentally capable of managing multiple projects and diverse teams are a real asset. It is not just the academic reach but the ability to take capacity into action.

Capacity is not just the organisation structure and its skill set. It needs to have the energy and spirit to drive into so-called unknown territories. Again, it is all about the people, the individuals who lead, and the teams that they build.

7. Attitudes, Motivation, and Systems

The organisational psyche is the fuel for action that moves the organisation with intrinsic and extrinsic programs that create excitement and growth at all levels. Motivation requires energy, and there are many programs that can create the require excitement to keep energy levels and spirits high and focused. Leadership charisma is certainly a plus, but is quickly overshadowed by great, innovative, compelling strategy. It is often thought that people resist change, but I think that this is more about poor change strategies and force-fed programs. Everything starts with great attitude, and although attitudes can change quickly by individuals and teams, this can be countered by creating environments based on fairness, respect, and opportunity to learn formally and informally. This brings both individuals and teams together in many collaborative ways. A culture built on learning and improvement as a base will support individual and team development. An organisation is in a continual state of learning from internal and external programs and experiences. As individuals develop from sponsored programs and environments, they feel more valued and motivated to contribute more of their value back to the organisation. It is a normal occurrence for people to want to repay back for benefits that they have received. This is often referred to as the power of obligation.

A great amount of effort is put into reward programs that are measured with hard data. Although important to the continuance of the organisation, performance alone does not reward all the inputs that are necessary to meeting the demands of achieving a great visionary goal. Organisations that have only hard, measured reward programs leave themselves vulnerable to copycat programs from their opposition or from organisations that are truly employers of choice. The leader needs to ensure that the emotive needs of the organisation are met through recognition, welfare, and individual development programs that see the leader understanding the importance of both the individual and team contribution and ensure that the organisations develop to have the capacity to meet the demands of great vision programs currently and in the future. The leader needs to be recognised as one of the team in terms of working together to the same committed end, but in leading, the teams from above need to ensure that all support, logistics, resources, and feedback in formal and informal recognition programs are available for the teams, and that they support individuals in performing their required roles at the right time and level. Such optimisation of the organisation requires great belief in the vision and its people and drives cooperative capability of all the individual teams.

I cannot overemphasise the importance of training, clear and concise communication, and 360-degree informal feedback for recognising contribution and contributors as motivating fuel for the organisation. As such, 360-degree performance or reviews should be an informal approach, such as when critiquing, ask for feedback on how you could have approached an issue or program differently. This requires strong agreed values to have been set. Formal, secret, 360-degree programs can be handled in a toxic manner and politically motivated. I have witnessed some terrible abuse in such a program. People need to be valued and should never be put in a situation where they can be manipulated or bullied.

8. Development and Succession

Leaders and their teams have only a limited tenure in comparison to the life of the organisation and the relative short term of leadership for its leader. Development and its succession are vital and should be a normal evolution rather than the revolutionary changes of leadership that seem to become a norm with theatrical fixes. Leaders who take such drastic approaches tend to have a limited vision, or the organisation is left in such a drastic and drained state that it leaves little scope for visionary leadership and requires hard management programs to get it back on a stable platform for growth and leadership. This may require a few leaders over relatively brief time periods to achieve a dynamic and strategic organisation ready for a visionary leader.

Succession planning at all senior levels is required, and nominating likely candidates and offering development programs to have them ready should the opportunity arise is prudent. As mentioned, leaders can have high opinions of themselves, and they can nominate successors who in their view have a likeness to themselves in character and attributes, or who come from similar backgrounds or disciplines, or who demonstrate attributes and characters that the leaders would like to see in themselves. Although this might be comforting, it may not be offering the organisation the right skill sets to take it to the next level with consideration to the internal and external forces that the organisations need to meet in order to move forward. External candidates should also be considered to ensure the organisation does not become myopic, but team fit is crucial to the culture. No matter how great the individual may seem, if they are not a cultural fit, then cooperation within the teams will be at risk. This is not to say that there is never conflict, because high-performance teams generate this. However, personal conflict can bring about bitterness that can rob the organisation of its natural momentum.

The key consideration for succession and understanding its importance is that the leader should have a vision which has reached well past her own individual tenure. This is a clear statement that the leader is about the organisation more so than herself. The leader should be a beneficiary of her own leadership.

9. Delegation and Empowerment Programs

Clear and transparent operating parameters and the definition of roles need to be on record (i.e., written), giving licence to managers and individuals to operate with clear boundaries that are able for all to understand and adhere to. Many managers tend to rely on great titles that are ambiguous and give no idea as to what their key roles are. Therefore, it is only sensible that that their roles are clearly circulated and that the boundaries of their operation and whom they report to and collaborate with to achieve their objectives are available. These role descriptions need to be well-circulated for all to have an understanding of what is to be achieved and where support can be given in terms of cross-collaboration and cooperation throughout the organisation. Leaders need to play a key role in articulating and keeping this information current. The human resource executive should be a support to the leader with this. Another approach is to form cross-collaboration with different skill sets and characters being given projects that force collaboration and hopefully innovative contribution. This is also an opportunity to test prospective leaders operating outside their normal skill sets and comfort zones.

Empowerment is not about anarchy but trust and openness to explore and improve processes and systems for the continual improvement of the organisation. Policy and operating practices need to be clearly articulated and reviewed regularly to keep up with the progress and development of the organisation. A process for their review by all needs to be established and can be as simple as an improvement or suggestion box. Many organisations use third-party consultants for sourcing organisation improvements and operating feedback; this can be beneficial because it is perceived as less threatening.

In delegating, the leader needs to manage the spans of control because the wider the span the less control and the greater the trust and sub-leadership needs to be. The wider span can lead to greater innovation, but the leader needs to ensure that all are on course.

10. Systems and Processes

All organisations consist of processes and systems. The hood is a system which operates out of a system of systems and its processes. The hood's system comprises infrastructure, technological software and hardware, organisational structure, and products and services, but it must operate within legal systems and rely on supply systems, marketing systems, and more. Within these systems are the processes that direct how all the components of a system operate to deliver the system's objective. If a clock is a system to tell the time, it has algorithms that could be viewed as processes, and if one fails, then the system is faulty or broken. Machine-driven systems are very consistent while working, and they rely on maintenance processes to keep them so. People are problematic in that they need to comprehend action processes to bring about the expected outcome. The issue at hand is that they are well-articulated and subject to continual review. Continuous improvement programs have been around in the modern management world, but technology has quickened the need for their review and so-called improvement. Having great processes and systems is often seen as the hallmark of successful management, but as a component of continuous improvement and innovative step changes, the least that there is and the simpler the operating processes are will make it easier for the organisation to have them well-actioned and engaged with employees. I have seen complex processes that are merely form over function and never thoroughly implemented. The message here is to keep them simple and open to improvement. Technology and improved education programs will continually bring change. Technology may bring about step change, and this may require a complete review of the processes and systems over the current way of doing things.

The key with process and systems management is to recognise that it is a critical approach to improving quality and culture in dynamic environments that people must implement and manage.

11. Procedures and Policies

Procedures and policies need to be succinct and relevant to establish employee boundaries and operating guidelines. There is a fear that articulation of operating procedures inhibits innovation, but this is only the case in an organisation that does not listen to itself and is not open to continuous learning and improvement. In some cases, the leader becomes so obsessed and self-centric with himself that he thinks he needs to solve every issue rather than embody the key role of implementing solutions from within the organisation and empowering the organisation to get on with what it should know needs to be done. There is no fast rule; rather, it's being open to what is best for the organisation and trusting the hood to operate within the guidelines and principles of its policies and within its values.

In developing policy, an organisation that participates in crafting them will more likely follow its policies and continue to contribute to its improvement. Clearly defined responsibilities and accountabilities avoid conflict and misunderstanding as to who does what and when. The golden rule is to keep instructions simple and brief rather than producing forms that are more for show than substance. Transparency as to who has responsibility and measured accountability for what is critical for rapid responses and keeping on track.

Policies are for guidance on how things are to be done for the moment and the foreseeable future, but they need to have the flexibility to be revised or rescinded because all context changes.

12. Information and Technology-driven Systems

Trust cannot be obtained without a responsible level of transparency as to the position, direction, and health of the organisation. The communication presentation needs to cater to all its audience rather than being caught up in academia and financial types of presentations that may be impressive in detail and results but that struggle to deliver the messages to all. This particularly applies to the financial department with reams of historical data but rarely an explanation of why the measures are so important, and it fails in recognising the contributors and its progress to the vision, which I believe can derail the hood's focus on its strategy. Much of the organisation needs to know that it is on track and that contributions are making a positive difference. Embracing technology is vital, and innovative programs and awareness is needed to keep at the frontier of the operating environment, but timing and relevance to the organisation is an important consideration for the leadership teams rather than newer technology as the only fix.

Technology enables timely reach to all and allows for accessibility for those entitled and those interested in its review and application for efficiency and effectiveness. Confidentiality is always a consideration, and this should be stated as so, but what is general in terms of strategy and performance should be made available with at least the next milestone to be labelled for purpose and action. Gone are the days of managers or leaders holding back information as a form of power and using its delivery for their own exposure and self-promotion. This should apply to the IT departments as well as a challenge to keep electronic processes as simple as possible.

Speed in delivery of communication is a contemporary challenge because if you don't present the information expediently, someone else might—and it may not be in keeping with the facts, or it could be taken out of context and create confusion as to what is the performance or go-forward strategy. The IT teams should have mechanisms in place to deal with this challenge, and they need to be a key contributor to the senior leadership team. Without careful management and distribution of information, beliefs can form that have no basis in fact.

Operationally, the IT team should have a clear appreciation of the operational constraints and challenges because any simplification of the operating environment will make the organisation more fluid.

Be aware that the introduction of innovative technology and IT-led programs can change the very shape of the organisation in its structure and skill sets that are required. The leader needs to ensure that any change is fit for purpose with the organisation's evolution in mind rather than a surprising coup or revolution that is outside strategy and vision.

There is a big case for leadership review on managing specialist departments or groups, and I think that a smaller executive span, although more hierarchical, would ensure that they are more synergistic than competing forces and that accessibility of relative information is available.

The digitalisation of organisations will be a very powerful resource for leaders who embrace this technology for all strategic benefits, but particularly for supporting a learning organisation that is capable of leading in this new world environment. This resource or emerging resource should not be confused with the roles of the people in the organisation. The primary role of IT is to manage information systems, disseminate, and provide simple tools for managers and leaders to make decisions from. Many an IT strategy has been to concentrate on reducing headcounts rather than strategic growth and wider customer interfaces.

13. Brand Management

Image

The leader is the custodian and representative of the organisation's image and brand, both inspirationally and in its current perception and form, as managed across all stakeholders and those who are on the future radar. The image and its reflection should belong to the organisation and not the leader's personal mantra. Many new leaders come into an organisation and lose its history through changing or reinventing the brand based on their own perception or designing it for their own self-promotion. All the leader's leadership and the actions of the organisation at mass and individual levels will impact the image in positive and negative connotations. In both forms, it can be strategic and or politically driven.

The leader is responsible as the steward for the brand, and its culture should not overlook the power and memorability of symbols. These can be contemporised without losing the essence of the brand, its purpose, and its history. This needs to be closely managed because perceptions can quickly become reality.

Industry Image

No organisation operates alone, and it needs to have the trust of those who work with the organisation to deliver on its mission.

Personal Image

The charisma of the leader can be hard to define, but it is required for the initial attention when selling the vision for the organisation. The leader needs to be able to engage and tell the story of where the organisation is going and why.

Community Image

There are moral and legal issues for consideration for the long-term sustainability of the organisation and its standing within the community. Future resources and patronage will be drawn from the community, and the HR strategies should deploy programs to be the employer of choice and develop employees for future success in all roles. Any strategy to build a positive image in the community needs to be real rather than patronising.

14. Corporate and Cross-team Complexities

Shared services or collaboration on whatever scale, and its interaction, contribution, and interference, is an important responsibility for the leader to manage in understanding what is going on, whether a corporation or third-party support in smaller organisations. It is the leader's responsibility to ensure that there is collaboration and cooperation across the teams, and that those resources are being applied to the teams in line with the strategy and its performance expectations. In larger organisations, there can be a corporate culture that needs to be understood for the leader's organisation to benefit from and remain in that corporation. Leaders of divisions can become corporate victims falling foul or out of favour of the good intentions of corporate support teams.

There is always plenty of good intention—or should we call it support?—that may be counter to the strategy and the vision. Some is imposed, such as corporate governance, compliance, and regulation, which maintains stability in keeping with external forces such as legislation and changing community standards. It is important to satisfy these and to not allow them to create misdirection through overexuberance in managing them by specialist managers.

By function, different teams within an organisation are comprised of different skill sets, and they exist with an informal pecking order which can be circumstantial or political, given the leader or the team's charisma. Teams are an outcome of strategic inputs, and if there is a need to change, the effect must be understood and must touch everyone on the team for a successful transition.

We tend to think about individual conflicts and misfits without thinking about the roles and the power plays that teams bring. It can be a healthy addition to the strategy execution, or it can actively work for their own benefit or at cross-purposes to their compatriot teams. Conflict and tension can be as healthy as it is disruptive and or destructive.

This leads to control and effect, and a leader is more likely to be successful with all the resources required to achieve his vision without having to be submissive to corporate board "support", because there is usually a price to be paid in some form that may compromise the progress to the vision.

15. Learning

Much has been written about learning organisations, and I have stressed that leadership is all about driving change. Change is happening all around internally and externally, and apart from being aware and having the ability to adapt to changes, it is necessary for an organisation to be a leader type and stay on mission. It will need to innovate and be so bold to become a catalyst of change, bringing itself to greater learning and innovation as successful change is innovation. This takes a leader with courage to challenge and manage through change and support the evolution, which is a positive consequence of a learning organisation. The learning organisation occurs at an individual level, and a leader needs to understand and appreciate that diversity brings opportunities for innovation that challenges and develops learning programs.

Succession is a key component of long-term vision, and internal and external training programs are important. I believe that reliance on arm's-length training and personal development in an organisation can impose unaligned beliefs in ideology and process on the desired organisation's culture, and these need to be balanced and managed. Be wary of the well-intentioned idealists that offer education that is against the organisation's strategy and culture. The point here is that the leader needs to be close to this, but the benefit is real.

Leaders need to have a capacity for self-criticism and allow analysis of their decisions to be debated so that they can learn for the improvement and progression of the strategy and allow involvement for its teams to actively achieve the vision. Too often, success creates an environment that leads to stagnation towards any further improvement and innovation, which leaves it vulnerable to the competition and a lack of progressive growth. This can lead to a situation where the senior team starts to doubt the leader, and a political destructive climate emerges. This discontent will impact the organisation's progress and distract the leader. Having a capacity for self-analysis and organisational review requires a great amount of maturity and transparency as to its purpose of improvement and innovation rather than seeing such analysis and review as a witch-hunt. Being an innovative progressive organisation requires a realisation that mistakes are part of the growth and that how they are dealt with is part of the learning progress. This needs to be an internal-driven system rather than outside looking in, and once instituted, it becomes a powerful and efficient improvement program. Outside looking in consultants and institutions are given great credibility, but their recommendations and assessment need to be given the same rigour as those of the internal reviews. Internal reviews need to be aware of perceptions because these can be convenient and politically pitched as facts, rather than the reality of candour and fact-based leadership that can put its own decision-making (and that of its teams) to the test of open, transparent debate. The leader needs to be aware of the noisy minority groups or the very articulate individual (whom I call the radio voice) who can be outspoken with bold propaganda in raising views that may conflict with strategy or views of the current position. This needs to be dealt with one way or another because they are raised with a purpose that lacks the holistic review that the leader and the hood should have.

This is not about whether an organisation should be a learning organisation, but that learning happens at many levels and has many angles. The thoughts and capability of the organisation needs to be understood and appreciated.

Learning occurs at an individual level but is applied at an organisational level.

EXTERNAL ISSUES

1. Acquisitioned Growth

Multichannel management, diversification, or the taking of a greater market share are leadership considerations that require capital but also require the way for all to integrate and have the management teams and resources that can capitalise on such a rapid influx of growth which may require a review of previous processes. However, with any acquired organisation, there are new teams that challenge what is with a clash of differing culture, systems, and policies that need to be managed. As in a two-horse race, there will be a winner, and rather than one group taking over another, the leader needs to take the best practices and create a new, improved culture which should be stated as a sought-after benefit of the acquisition. Acquisitioned growth is a benefit of immediate scale, but it needs careful management because there is a clash of culture and systems, and an objective review needs to ensure the best of all is applied while the whole organisation moves through positive change to that of a new organisation. Leaders need to be aware of the resistance to change and the jockeying for new and more responsible leadership and management positions. Acquisition growth also brings along an opportunity for further organic growth and overall operational improvement. Do not miss the learning opportunities and the innovation that could be at hand before individual and team politicking squashes the opportunity to do so.

2. Compliance Management

An over-zealous approach to compliance can cause a defection from the strategy and can work against improving culture if managed as compliance for compliance's sake rather than tackling it strategically for system improvement and becoming a better organisation. Compliance and its intent should be envisioned in the vision and its strategy. The hood needs to be compliant, but how it is applied is critical because it needs to be viewed as a value-adding process in the hood's operations and strategy build in achieving the vision. Compliance is to be expected, but it is to be always open for challenge in its application. There needs to be a policy that facilitates this because there needs to be encouragement and recognition for any suggestion that improves the organisation's strategy in compliance and its systems.

External compliance programs can be challenging to fit into the operating and capital management programs for organisations with compliance to governance, environmental, OH&S, and legislative programs that must be adhered to.

The leader needs to ensure compliance at a mandatory level is met and then balance improvement-generating programs against overly unnecessary compliance. Greater bureaucracy brings little benefit.

3. Competitive Reaction

Competitors will and should always react. This can be an endorsement of the leader's strategies and may result in market pressure, but that is the way of free markets. The leaders need to ensure that strategy is on track and is not bumped by competitors emulating what has occurred. With continuous improvement and learning, the organisation can innovate and grow while maintaining its niche.

The key approach should be to be aware of your competitors and your organisation's position against them. At all times, the emphasis should be on your customers or those that generate the benefit to your organisation and improvements to them and your own operating efficiencies.

4. Supplier Relationships

Maintain results and a winner status with the valued support of suppliers. Suppliers are critical, and it is vital to view them as allies or reverse customers rather than being treated as adversaries. Too often, overly aggressive leadership or zealous purchasing managers can destroy a relationship for the sake of a short-term advantage. The trade-off is to give the supplier an offsetting advantage such as increased sustainable volume. The leader's endorsement of the supplier should include the value of the product, the level of service sought, and the supplier's culture. A good saying regarding any relationship is, "Lay down with dogs, and you will catch fleas." You may not have the opportunity to be the supplier's biggest customer, but you should strive to be the most valued partner. Many buyers don't treat their suppliers as strategic partners, missing the value benefits outside of the direct relationship with their products and services. Taking a leadership approach will seek access to the additional strategic intelligence, skills, and wide networks that can be of great strategic benefit. The leader needs to have presence up and down the value chain to understand all opportunities and threats that lead to their organisation benefiting from all opportunities that such networking and external collaboration can bring. It is a very powerful relationship when you can agree on shared visions and strategies with suppliers and distributors that are of joint benefit and have a joint will to achieve. This increases the skill set and strategic resources for the leader's organisation. The results for both will become a natural output and enabler for both organisations' cultures to function effectively and efficiently, with wins for all up and down the value chain.

5. Customers

No one has more customers than the leader, and in many cases, the leader will be dealing with other leaders who represent many customers. In preparing vision and strategy, I have spoken about the benefit of being a motivation for action, and customers should be seen as beneficiaries of the organisation's vision and strategy. Segmentation of customers allows for targeting the most suitable customers for your organisation. No organisation can have 100 per cent market share, and neither should it aspire to be; the further the reach, the higher the cost. Lowering of effect can be a negative to overall performance. Customers pay well with their hard-earned money and advocacy, using their scarce time to benefit from the hood. The organisation expends a lot of resources in satisfying customers, and they should be future loyal promoters of the organisation. In understanding customers and their attitudes towards the organisation, I recommend the use of the Net Promoter Score (NPS) program. Also, the collection of verbatim comments from customers is very concise, relevant feedback. Circulate them to all the relevant customer interfaces within the organisation to understand what is being delivered. Then strategically react to them in order to continually and constantly improve customer loyalty and promotion of the organisation.

A leader should promote the same customer-related attitudes and behaviours across the organisation when dealing with all beneficiaries of the organisation up and down its value chain. This is one of the behaviours that leaders can impose in the organisation through their own examples. All people who add value to the organisation should be highly regarded, respected, and treated as customers. It is amazing how an organisation can be transformed into a high-performance one with customer-centric leadership. Customers are so wonderful and cost effective in growing businesses, and it is amazing that it is often not spoken about as a leadership priority.

6. Shareholders

Boards and shareholders have grand expectations that are primarily financial but should be viewed as beneficial for the organisation's performance and vision. Boards need to be very aligned to the vision and supportive of the leader of the time whom they have empowered on behalf of its shareholders (owners). Shareholders are the dictators of the share price and impact board decisions, and their belief in the organisation is paramount. Performance is an indicator of an organisation's health, but confident communication and understanding amongst all stakeholders will benefit an organisation through trying times. Boards need to play a stronger role regarding the new digital communication environment in talking to and updating their shareholders. They should take on the leadership behaviours as well for their own strategy in supporting the leader's vision.

Although very influenced through the financial performance, boards have wide-ranging responsibilities that protect the organisation from any penalty that is usually financially based, whether by fines or by community and customer disenfranchising.

Leaders need to focus on the inputs and imagery (i.e., brand symbolism) that deliver the benefits to shareholders. Performance and strategy need to stay in balance to maintain leadership tenure.

MANAGEMENT

B EING CHALLENGED BY VARIOUS leadership styles, objectives, and rivalry amongst their peers and competitive forces creates a chaotic environment in which managers function and compete to fulfil their own missions.

Before considering the steps of leadership required to achieve the vision and its objectives, it would be remiss to not mention the importance of management and its practices. A leader will need to have and rely on management teams to execute, deliver on the strategy, and measure its progress. Management needs to work on the businesshood environment to deliver on all fronts of the strategy. Leadership and management is crucial to the operating environment, which is paramount in delivering and improving the organisation. It is the leader who has the responsibility to deliver the resources, systems, and structure in order to create the best strategic pathway to the vision.

Often a lot of resource is applied to making people and their teams greater, but thought should be given to making the environment a better or simpler one for the average person or team to be great in, rather than trying to make great people in a confused operating environment.

Senior management communication is often an area that can be complex and requires definition to ensure that the right message has been understood. Senior management is crucial to energising and leading their teams to achieve their specific objectives in synchronicity with the other groups, with the direction of the organisation's leader.

All managers need to have some leadership skills, but they have the advantage of being supported by the leader and being cross-functional with other associated management groups and supportive stakeholders within the businesshood. Remember that external stakeholders are considered members of the hood.

With management being critical to the execution and measurement, what does the leader do? Leading and managing. Managers may be part of the role, but more important, the role is to adapt and adjust the strategy and the vision to changes within and outside of the hood, whether by design or not. Leaders must also drive changes that are productive, efficient, and beneficial for the businesshood. This leads to thinking about the saying, "Working on the business rather than working in the business." This then beggars the question: Who supports the leader, and does leadership operate within a team or outside of the team? That references all the skills of their management teams and stakeholders of the businesshood. Does the leader consider himself as part of the team?

Organisationally, this can create a separation between the leader and the senior management groups. This separation of roles and responsibilities is what creates the tension that is required to bring about high performance. Therefore, successful leadership is incumbent on the businesshood's teams and management, as well as the supportive direction and resource given to those teams. Leaders tend to have a wide-reaching view of where the businesshood impacts and benefits. This insight includes understanding the competition and positioning the organisation for leveraged benefit, being the most effective and productive that it can be.

DECISION-MAKING

P ROBLEMS CAN BE LIKENED to a pie that consists of many slices. Tackle one slice at a time, and soon it will be manageable. It's a simple analogy, but it's a simple divide-and-conquer process that can have teams working on key decisions. Leaders should not overlook the opportunity for cross-functional collaboration in tackling issues. Leaders have an uncanny ability to see problems in a different light, and therefore they need to remain aware of the emotions that may exist within their organisations when their teams are faced with problems and need to be supported on all levels in order to manage through them.

Where appropriate, problems and issues should be dealt with openly with reasonable and responsible transparency. Too often, not enough effort is applied throughout an organisation under a false understanding that there is no problem or issue, and all is fine. Beware—this denial could be political. There can be a tendency for some managers and teams to engage in happy talk to hide or deny that there is a problem that needs to be addressed, or it is outside of their scope of competency, and they cover their inadequacy.

Gaining consensus is always preferred, but there will be times that the leader will need to make a call, whether based on instinctive judgement or fact due to necessity. These calls are the very reason for leaders, rather than best managers who may rely on more formal decision-making approaches.

Leadership can be referred to as an art rather than the more theoretical aspects of management. This can explain the insightful decision-making that leaders tend to make following a more holistic appreciation of the situation at hand. It addresses the downstream impact of the decision and its ongoing relationship to the business's direction and objectives. In stating the above, I do not mean to underplay the requirement for the leader to have a full appreciation on the organisation's performance and position when making decisions or deciding who should be given such a task. Maybe the insightfulness has more to do with when you need to decide who should be involved in the process of the decision, how the solution is to be implemented, and by who.

Management decision-making can be very analytical and based on form or process and systems that are in place or evolving. It is very different to the directness and snappiness of executive leadership decision-making. Executive leadership and its decision-making is based on a clear understanding of direction and trust in the teams that its leads.

In influencing or seeking a decision, you need to understand the personality and psychology of whom you are trying to influence. I knew one senior manager who would feel comfortable only in executing a solution when he felt he had solved it or had not been pressured to do so. In this case, I would only give him half a solution or an idea of one, and I'd let him incubate the problem with a pathway for a solution. I'd continue to prod until he decided on a completed agreeable solution. In having solved the problem, he would lead and execute with vigour.

The key point is that if you do not have the power to execute, you need to have a personal strategy for influence to implement your need.

STRATEGIC VALUES

L EADERS NEED TO SET and develop the values of the business, the
personal interactions amongst the teams, and the values imparted and
contributed to the communities from which it operates and benefits.
Values need to be propagated because the values will set attitudes and
behaviours, which will set the culture of the organisation. These values need
to be consistent and value adding to the strategy execution. These values
should be the organisation's guidelines and rules for engagement within
the organisation, as well as operating outside with external stakeholders and
within the communities that support the business and its brand.

PERSONAL

These values need to be agreed by the organisation and referred to
when team members engage with each other on the principles of truth
and transparency, tempered with empathy and respect, with the mission
of implementing the strategy and achieving its vision. Having established
personal values opens the door to dealing with issues and respecting others
without losing the purpose of the groups and how performance will be
accessed and monitored, as well as the way the business teams interact
with one another. These values are very important because guidelines
can protect not only the hood but also the individual with clear direction,
avoiding such things as conflicts of interest.

BUSINESS

Business values set the platform for team members' engagement with third-party stakeholders such as suppliers and community. Integrity and fairness are base rules to a respectfulness, which will bring on more supporters for the vision and the operating success of the business. These will be very consistent with the brand values but address internal issues as well. The business values need to set out the golden rules for integrity, open communication, fairness, and forums for dealing with conflicts and how all team members are valued and have a voice in suggesting or criticising programs without fear. They have an understanding that consensus and the leader's direction is to be followed providing they meet both personal and business values.

COMMUNITY

Organisations leverage off their local communities, and therefore there is an obligation and a beneficial moral responsibility to support and add value back into the community with respect to its legislative laws and traditions, without interfering with its make-up or being distracted from its objectives. There may be times where the businesses resources are required by the greater community.

SUPPLY CHAIN

An organisation's values can be at risk if it collaborates and deals with organisations that do not share similar values. Do not confuse values with multi culturalism. There can be differences, but they should not compromise the values of your own organisation. Any compromise will open the door for further compromise and deterioration of your own values. "Lay down with dogs, and you will catch fleas."

Sharing values develops an espirit de corps amongst all stakeholders, building trust and an understanding of roles and the importance of their service and contribution with a holistic, winning team focused on achieving the organisation's goals.

MEDIA ———————————————————————

Beware of handing your organisation over to assessment or opinion from organisations that can communicate messages, opinions, and scrutiny through any type of medium outside of your control. You need to have a strategy and policies in place regarding whom and how they deal with outside communicators who have wide reaches. The digital environment can communicate rapidly, but the question is what to communicate. Manage your communication before someone else does.

When dealing with media organisations, your organisation's values (and your own) will be put to the test. I am not saying to avoid the media, but be aware of their power and reach and have a clear strategy on why you are dealing with them.

ATTITUDES AND BEHAVIOURS

WHAT YOU INSPIRE, DO, and allow is what you teach. The leadership issue is all about setting the scene and showing an example for performance and behaviour. This can be a challenge because it may require organisational changes and the selection of new members, teams, and current stakeholders. The saying "Hire the attitude and teach the skill" can be more relevant than the perfect resumé.

Attitudes and behaviours can be communicated through the purpose of the vision and the excitement of progressive achievement as the organisation reaches its milestones and celebrates at every relevant opportunity.

Motivational programs, both intrinsic and extrinsic, are important in shaping behaviour and growth. Become an organisation of choice with all rewards based on those beneficiaries at all levels as an outcome of the performance and individual or team contribution. Such adherence to the strategy and its vision needs to apply across all areas that associate with and impact the businesshood. This is where leadership should be artful as well as technical in direction, for overarching understanding of the businesshood's sphere of influence and gainfulness.

There are many programs that human resource practitioners have at their disposal for testing likely attitudes, but leadership presence and feedback on performance are powerful shaping mechanisms. The morale of the organisation is so important, and leaders need to constantly sense this and modify their own behaviours and approaches based on the morale of individuals, groups, and the organisation.

What you allow will soon become the norm. What you teach and what you sow is what you reap.

MOTIVATION

E MOTION IS SUCH AN important aspect of great leadership because a leader will lead individuals, not teams. People form teams themselves even within the structured, functional teams that managers and leaders put together. When to apply emotion-driven motivation programs over a non-emotive program is a decision practice that is about the development of motivated people who apply themselves to their specific actions of achieving the strategy. With the right direction and support, the people will form the teams that are required. This is the basis of motivated human behaviour to contribute and move to cross-functional collaboration of teams, which has many performance and cultural benefits to achieve the objective. Be aware that there will be those who, whether intentionally or not, work against the strategy and the formulation or evolution of the natural, high-performance teams. These high-performance teams will also exist within the informal organisational structure as well as their formal organisational formation. There will be managers who cannot accept informal teams because they feel it is a lessening of their own control, power, or importance.

To motivate people to the objective, the tasks at an individual level need to be accepted. This involves emotive communication, leading by example, and lots of excitement with the benefit of personal and team reward, whether intrinsic or extrinsic. The organisation needs to have belief that all is within their capability and is acceptable to their personal values as well as the business values.

The leader will need to be able to balance the clear, factual decision-making required with the ability to simplify and deliver plans that the majority can understand and progressively work with. The reward process is very important and needs to be timely. Performance graphics can assist the communication to those who do not require all the detail over which senior management may be obsessing. This can be achieved using simple desktop dashboards, with the skill being to select the right, meaningful, key performance indicators. Also, scorecards, which not only track performance progress but benchmark against comparable organisations without losing sight of the vision, are helpful in establishing the can-do attitudes that are necessary.

The keyword is belief, and this can overcome the trepidation of striving towards great goals and accepting innovative ways of working. The right motivation and direction will lead to very positive behaviours that culminate into a powerful and productive culture.

CULTURE

A FISH ROTS FROM THE head. This is an analogy aptly applicable for disparate organisations because poor culture is caused or advocated by the leader, whether knowingly or not. The leader is responsible for what the culture is and what it aspires to become. Behavioural standards need to be stated in policy and with overstated examples from all, from the leader down, who can have the opportunity to influence and develop aligned, enduring, and supportive cultures. The issue with understanding culture is that it exists with a multitude of subcultures based on individuals, teams, and the organisation's position in its many contexts, as well as an individual's experiences, rather than being imposed from a presentation of the organisation's vision and strategy. To its benefit, culture is not static. It is dynamic and adaptive to all the perceived messages, inputs, and outputs of the organisation. Therefore, such a dynamic must be nurtured by the leader with leadership by example, not a case of "Do as I say, not what I do," by clearly stating behavioural norms and being transparent with communication whether it is good or unwelcome news. The positive in delivering unwelcome news is that the audience is likely to trust all future communication as being real, and they feel they are worthy of the information being shared with them. It is very important to recognise that individual and group subcultures can coexist and contribute to an overarching, positive, supportive culture focused on the hood's strategic vision. The hood is a collective, and the astute leader will use all the positive aspects of everyone and the subcultures to the advantage of achieving the vision. Interfering with personal culture will bring resistance.

The leader needs to introduce a new businesshood's culture for the teams and individuals to contribute in a positive way. This is not replacing individual beliefs but will give guidance as to how the hood will operate and behave with respect to supporting personal differences while having absolute focus on the mission at hand to achieve the vision. Managers will insert key performance indicators (KPIs) into the organisation to measure behavioural progress (e.g., turnover, conflict resolution and grievances, absentees). The leader needs to continually reinforce the vision for the culture to adapt and embed itself into the organisation to get a feeling as to what is really happening. This can be as simple as weekly morning teas, having one-on-one discussions, and keeping an ear tuned to other conversations. This overarching culture cannot be successful if it is at odds with any of the other subsets. This is more than likely an issue that the leader and the organisation will need to deal with time and time again. New additions to the organisation needs to be selected on their fit, as well as the skills that they can bring to the organisation. HR managers often refer to team fit, but this needs to also be considered with organisation fit and aptitude to aligning with the organisation's vision. Culturally, you need contribution but also advocacy.

In today's world, this can be further complicated by geographic boundaries and their cultural differences. Again, the leader's task is to keep the vision well-articulated and understood against all the differences that exist, and that direction is understood with simple execution and timely feedback. A great amount of management effort is put towards the so-called management of such diversity that manifests from gender, sexual preference, religion, ethnicity, age, and more. The leader should manage within the laws to have the best groups and individuals rather than balancing the so-called diversity books, without overlooking the benefits that can be had from leading very diverse teams to achieve the vision and its objectives. Bringing differences together is a precursor to delivering innovation. In having a great business culture, many expect harmony, but the hood needs energy. A great culture will have tension but will deal with it using mature, goal-oriented solutions. This has been termed by some as "storming and performing."

Understanding the significant cultural drivers is the essence to understanding how to best influence and direct the group efforts and establish their trust, belief, and stamina to go the distance with you. Culture is the sum of and the basis of individual and group behaviours, and as is the case in any organisation, people make the difference no matter how poor or great the strategy and its management. All my discussion has been to focus on leadership, but management is not to be overlooked because they lead, execute, and run the field teams, dynamically adjusting to internal and external influencers. A key role of the leader is to support the management teams to strategically perform.

Embedded in culture are politics and personal ambition, which needs to be managed with transparency and investing with development of the individual and groups for an alignment with the strategy. This development is to occur at every level and with such opportunity that exists in a learning organisation. The astute leader will optimise the learning opportunities at every area of the businesshood, and that is conducive to the purpose and objectives of the hood.

Culture being the sum of all behaviours, all aspects of the communication and language of the strategy needs to appreciate the differences and areas of commonality that can be exploited. Involvement and feedback on performance can be an excellent ally for such challenges. The successful leader will have a very clear understanding of culture and the importance of his or her own integrity in bringing out the best in individuals and teams.

Do not underestimate the resistance and difficulty of changing culture. I would resist doing so without leading a trusted team in making bold, symbolic changes to alert all who may be working against the new leadership regime or who are in denial that change is required, and that past performance has not been acceptable or beneficial for the hood.

We talk about leadership in a singular sense, but we should be promoting a culture of leadership throughout an organisation, which is built upon the power of teams that display leadership traits individually and in group behaviours. This puts the primary leader in a position of service and support to achieve the vision.

STRUCTURE

T EAMS ARE CLEARLY FIT for purpose, and their structure should be an enabler for efficient and productive achievement to their goals and their support of the strategy for the achievement of the vision. The very word *structure* has one immediately think of departments of support teams and how the hood is designed to operate. The purpose of the structure is to efficiently and effectively achieve the objectives of the vision and the mission, supporting the leader's strategy while satisfying the legislative and financial requirements of the organisation. The structure needs to maintain flexibility, and this is best managed through narrower spans and hierarchical management control. Leaders who trust their great teams can have narrower spans but need to have the aptitude to reach deep into the organisation to remain in touch with the real culture and energy that is required to achieve great visions. There also needs to be acknowledgement of the informal structure that always exists; appreciate that their influences can cross functions that are well out of their expertise, with both positive and severe impacts on performance and culture. The stratification of the organisation needs careful attention because wide spans lose control and too many senior managers for a hood is the same as the old saying "Too many cooks spoil the broth." At the end of the day, someone (and this can be at varying levels) needs to be clearly in control for making the final decisions that move the teams and the organisation forward. A leader who understands the real factual needs will empower teams, make the decisions, and influence the required movement accordingly. There has often been clutter-causing conflict and ineffective progress with senior management, which stifles communication and action and misleads middle-level management, which in turn becomes at odds to supporting the leader and hence the vision.

Leaders usually have a direct involvement on the organisation's structure and the executives that makeup the structure. The leadership style and personality will have a role on the scope and span for the structure, the strategic imperatives that the organisation faces, and the power of the individual teams. The leader's style and abilities will have a direct impact on the make-up of the organisational structure, its hierarchy, and its span.

Specific role power can mislead the overall course of the strategy due to ever-widening spans of control and executive persona or style. It is worth mentioning some of the executive roles that can impact the strategy and the successful overall leadership of the organisation. When discussing structure and effective leadership, the debate seems to centre on the number of direct reports rather than the number of functions. Functions are becoming more of an issue as the professional scope of management becomes narrower, with specialisation and further complexity of roles creating a greater number of functional areas of contribution. Clear definition of roles and their accountabilities are vital and should be the licence for functional empowered management supporting sub-leadership and contribution within the business strategy and the scope of management. On the other hand, it should not inhibit cross-functional collaboration, broad development of team members, and support within the business. I understand that there is a requirement for specialists and like departments, and those should be clearly recognised and rewarded. However, they do not need to be given their own kingdoms over which to rule. Structure design should be about the departments of the business that are required to support and achieve the strategy requirements for the vision, rather than a cluster of specialist roles and departments. Many organisations are so great at managing their customers but do not recognise the customers within their own organisation by concentrating on control rather than influence and value.

Clear, simple, articulated roles with key performance objectives that are required for a functional guide for performance assessment should be available for all in the organisation to understand the responsibilities and reach of each function manager while encouraging cross-functional collaboration. The leader needs to be wary of any duplication or conflict that could arise. This leads to the design strategy for spans of control and hierarchy of control to ensure that course is maintained in order to reach milestones and align with the organisation's values, mission, and vision.

The leader has reach and control into every function but should support, not manage, the management of tactical objectives. A leader should ensure that the combined effort is conducive to the achievement of the progressive vision. A lot more of design thought for organising structure should be around leadership traits rather than the traditional sourcing of specialists at the higher levels of the organised hierarchy.

Successful leadership of the organisation should have the leader's mind applied to the overall support of moving the organisation to the achievement of the organisation's vision. This cannot be achieved by being too deeply involved in functional management. In devising structural models, this may require hierarchical management structures rather than wide spans of management teams or creating divisions with separate leadership within the organisation for more direct control over the processes to reach the strategic milestones for the ultimate vision.

This requires senior management teams to have strong leadership qualities in order to appreciate the strategic nature of achieving the vision while managing the complexities of their own responsibilities and objectives. The leader is responsible for the overall outcome and how this is achieved because he can give responsibility but not his own accountability.

The other consideration is to understand the level of resources and time that needs to be applied to key stakeholders, and how this can be done efficiently. Leaders need to work on the overall environment field for simple application to the organisation's tasks, rather than the complexity that management programs can bring about.

Active leadership does not necessary equate to great leadership. Many new leaders are very active in moving the chairs on the *Titanic* from one side to the other, but they do not check or change the course of the organisation to remain on strategy. The resetting of the organisational structure and replacing people is a very active and visual strategy which can become mere form over function. This can become a continuum by simply replacing people over time; the organisation has its own gravity, which will move back to its own comfortable water level without strategic leadership. Over time in some organisations, this is a circular condition that creates instability. This is a more frequent occurrence and shows the abusive power of such leadership, but it is likened to running up and down on the spot and it leeches talent to the competition and manifests into new emerging threats. The structure of an organisation is vitally important, but at its very core, it is made up of individuals. This leads back to the point that leaders lead individuals, not teams or organisations, and all strategy needs to be purposeful, have meaning, and be beneficial to them.

The human resource and its strategy is the machine that the leader uses to achieve the vision, and it needs to be resourced and directed for total optimisation down to every individual. The leader is supported by the human resource function, which manages the complexities of people in organisations and their support in compliant environments and legislative requirements. Any support or influence can be misread as power and needs to be carefully managed by the leader to ensure that strategy and direction are on track.

HUMAN RESOURCES

I N MANAGING THE COMPLEXITIES and idealism of organisations within all necessary compliances and confidentialities for the myriad of individual issues, organisational conflict and employee relationship strategies can place the human resource departments in powerful, influential roles in strategy involvement, but they are not operationally executable. This involvement can lead to frustration and overstepping of the human resource function. They can and should have a strong supportive role, at least in a motivational and articulated role. Their very nature of involvement at a team and individual level can be challenging with managing confidentialities, and they can also be misleading in giving advice on operational strategy and actions that are outside their skill source or current involvement within the organisation's leadership aspirations. They are involved in delivering motivational programs that are intrinsic and extrinsic to improve the operating and performance environment by providing the information and resources that recognise that people deliver the changes and that their teams are stronger than individuals.

Human resource counsel can be very helpful for the leader and should be free of the biases that can eventuate within teams that have operational responsibilities and goals, remembering that they are tribes competing in the hood and can have a bias in nominating individuals for leadership roles. There is an important, deep aspect of human resources that requires specialised management listening and clarity of aligning resources to the strategy by articulating and disseminating roles and their accountability. It requires great clarity to set roles that have separation but allow for a culture of cooperation and collaboration with overlapping, shared success factors while considering an overarching aim of locking into the vision. This is discussed in more detail because I think that there is a tendency for some HR departments to form into an idealistic police force rather than the much-required strategic support service for the organisation and its people that makes the teams, individuals, and their environment the best that they can be while remaining focussed on the vision.

In developing collaborating, strategic role descriptions, there should be a focus on developing a supportive satellite leadership structure operating around the visionary leader's beneficiary-led strategy, with the organisation's leaders orchestrating their efforts through support in the application and authorisation of resources, motivation, and results. There is not one function or role that I can think of that does not overlap or rely on another!

Individual development and counselling is a very important and sensitive aspect of the HR teams. Sourcing and growth of teams and people need to be embedded in the vision and strategy to focus human resources on the vision goals.

In larger organisations, the human resources team has a huge management agenda, supporting the strategy through the people resource and culture in order to embrace learning and create support across the hood, ensuring cooperation and competitive fairness in terms of remuneration, motivation, compliance, and succession for all the hood's operations. Human resource teams need to have a clear understanding of their administrative operational roles, and their strategic roles of ensuring the organisations human resources are supported and developed to keep pace with the forward challenges of the vision. The leader needs to be very aware of the selection and operational processes of the human resource effort. Acknowledging the importance of best management of its people through the leader's direct management or through direction of a human resource team will create the innovative resources necessary. This will ensure that they are made available and are the managers of tailored, targeted development programs and technology that improve the environment and individuals within the teams. In placing an emphasis on support leadership within the human resource team, we can place the HR team and its strategies at the cornerstones to growing the capacity and capability of the teams in order to make headway towards the ever-evolving vision.

Vision is about considering the future, and human resource leaders need to have strong supporting roles in ensuring that there is a solid structure for succession plans to be in place for continuity of culture and development growth for the ever-moving vision and the new leadership.

First, a vision may be too far-fetching or impractical. A vision needs to have a reasonable level of confidence regarding its do-ability. The human resource team is very important to the placement and development of the organisation's changing competencies, which are required along the pathway to achieving the organisation's visions and timetable.

The HR team has a more abstract role of developing the organisation to not only have the ability to achieve the vision but also have the competency and capability to manage after achievement of the vision and the leader's tenure. Too many new vision leaders—or rather, post-vision leaders—nuke the organisation's people and source a new team, which they believe has the capability to achieve their new vision. It is amazing to think that someone would want to lead an organisation that they do not trust. If culture is important, what has happened in the case of the nuking strategy? Harnessing an organisation's energy and competency would seem to be a more practical and efficient approach. Although every new leadership event has it challenges, there is a requirement for change. But of interest is understanding who the beneficiaries of the changes are and ensuring they are the most appropriate.

In discussing human resource, it is worthwhile to think about some of the HR measures that are driven in organisations. Their achievement is deemed as having been successful while opposed from the real achievement of the organisation's vision and strategy, let alone its immediate financial goals.

Diversity is an interesting one. Diversity is inherent in organisations with skills, age, gender, religion, education levels, ethnicity, and cultural differences. Putting aside any legislative requirements, all consideration should be given to the skill required, perceived fit to the team, and long term-likely contribution rather than forced decision-making for the achievement of idealistic, so-called management measures. Subcultures quickly emerge, and these can have their different agendas and ethics. In considering team fit, one of the stumbling blocks for an organisation is having a high turnover of people. This should be an alarming indicator that something is very wrong with the strategy, apart from its cost and loss of experience. A lot of human resource management effort is placed on developing and testing the culture. Defining a desired culture is where we get it wrong. That confuses the very benefit of having a diversified organisation. There needs to be a structure and policy on the behaviours of the individual regardless of any outside of the organisation differences. The emphasis needs to be on having a common purpose for why diverse people have been brought together. Again, the vision needs to be well-articulated and freely available, and any changes should be communicated in a timely manner. The new desired culture will follow as an outcome of strategy inputs.

It is very easy for the operations teams to call on the HR teams to manage disciplinary issues rather than take a more strategic approach towards creating a developing and nurturing organisation that is capable of meeting modern demands and achieving a high vision. This can have the HR team working in the business rather than the more strategic needs of developing the organisation's people and team capability in skills and belief in order to achieve the vision.

The human resources leader needs to be driven by the human resource strategy and should not become a resource for functional mangers to use at their convenience or as a cost benefit against their budgets.

OPERATIONS AND SALES

B EING RESPONSIBLE FOR THE day-to-day management of the business's execution of its strategy, operating within all policy, and optimising its performance is obviously a very powerful and sought-after role. Primarily it's a senior management role, and it should also be viewed as a prerequisite to having high leadership and collaborative skills because it is required in order to implement the ideas of others. I have had the very frustrating experience of working with several operation managers who have been more interested in their own selfish ego-managed positions and rewards than working cooperatively with support teams to achieve results. Operations requires strong individuals who can handle the rigours of such a critical, responsible role. When the business is performing well, they report the results; when it's not, they can try to deflect issues back into the organisation.

The problem here is that the vulnerable in the organisation will attach to them when performance is strong, and they'll avoid them for their own survival when it's not. In having such a singular view in managing the performance, they can tend to stifle innovation and promote group think. This can be a bottleneck for innovative, strategic growth and performance. The operations role can be so myopic due to the demands of the role that they miss out on their own growth, development, and this can lead to personal discontent, which can lead to a high turnover of managers in this role. There needs to be care that strategic communications are not funnelled through operations solely, because this can be very directive and misconstrued as the source giving the leader a distant context rather, than championing the open communication of programs, which should be inspirational, holistic, and engaging.

There is so much more for a business or an organisation to achieve than direct, measured operating performance. Many stakeholders are interested in other objectives within the organisation. Lime-lighting operations could appear as tactical achievement rather than the type of achievement for the hood to have a vision-driven, enduring future. It is worth noting that such a strong managerial role requires great leadership to create strategic, aligned, progressive performance. There could be a tendency for those focused on the short-term goals to forego innovation and change that could lead to it becoming uncompetitive or no longer relevant.

Managers may operate successfully separated from leadership traits, but leaders cannot set great management apart from good leadership. It is a double-edged sword that they must master. If leadership is so forward looking, there needs to be awareness to actions that interfere with successful, vision-driven leadership. The organisation can become a single point with a sole personality or overemphasised operations focus, and it can lose the overall, long-term vision that the leader had in mind. With such an emphasis on performance, there can be a loss of vision and the exclusion of stakeholders, businesshood responsibilities, and accountability, delivering short-termed, tactical performance. The operating environment uses a huge amount of energy and resources with a dominating profile that can be wrongly managed through negating the support and expertise of the greater organisation. This can be the battleground for internal conflict to arise over current performance being incongruent with the strategy and its vision.

There is no doubt that operational accountability is more current and performance orientated compared to those managers who may be charged with developing the foundations for the future as required in the vision. There cannot be a bright future without the operations of the business performing, but from a leadership perspective, we are discussing the future and optimising all aspects of the organisation. This does emphasise the need for the operations manager to have appreciation for the strategic purpose, and there needs to be a clear definition as to what is defined as operations. In some organisations this is sales, supply chain, or logistics, or a combination of functions.

In recognising that the operating management role is very high profile, dynamic, and flexible and is at the coal face of the organisation, it requires leadership direction and all the businesshood support with excellent listening and management. This is meant to capture and understand feedback on its performance and the market forces for strategic review and innovation to be dynamic with the total businesshood environment and its demands.

The leader, in guiding the application of all resources and their fair perception of their allocation, will need to work closely with the operating management and their teams to ensure that acknowledgement and respect within and for all the businesshood is managed. Otherwise it will be at the peril of an unaligned subculture emerging with an informal strategic application of the way the businesshood performs. While doing so, the leader needs to remain focused on the leadership aspirations rather than becoming an adjunct to the operation (sales) team. One set of functional goals is not to be put above the other collective functional goals to ensure the overall achievement of the vision.

One such subculture emergence causes a chain of disruption and division that is more than the weakest link because it propagates other sections of the businesshood to react with similar cultural and application breakdowns. This dilemma is often referred to as working in the business rather than working on the business. The operating environment is so intense that it requires immense focus, and therefore it requires such stringent leadership support and guidance to maintain and adapt the strategy with the vision always in mind.

Operations-driven organisations can be very visual because the control aspect is a very powerful one, but there is a lack of abstract in strategic thinking that stretches resources and isolates the organisation's overall talent and capacity.

Giving kudos for performance to the operations or sales teams without recognising the way-for-all given across the organisation can create a narrow-based management program that can milk the organisation's resources without the necessary investment to cope with future demands and required growth to cover the compounding costs within the businesshood. Referring and analysing completely to the businesshood considers the benefits that may be delivered from upstream in the supply chain from within and outside the hood.

Measures may be a key tool, and many organisations have combated these issues by developing a balanced score card focussing on inputs as well as outputs. Also, when performance is low, the leader must take accountability and action because the operations group cannot be used as a scapegoat. The leader always has overall accountability.

ENGAGEMENT

N<small>O MATTER HOW BIG</small> the team or group, there will be a greater proportion that is not as engaged with the strategy as it should be. It's like being at a sports game, and there are more spectators and commentators on the plays rather than those on the field who are striving to make the difference. The leader needs to be aware of the commentators but also acknowledge and support the players who will bring about the changes and results. Too often it is easy to be caught up with managing the commentary and the perceptions of the organisation's position rather than supporting those active managers who are performing to the strategy and driving subsequent performance. In these cases, beliefs can be very dominant but are not necessarily facts, and it is important to foster a culture that can handle and adjust to facts. A saying I have often used regardless of religious belief is, "In God I trust; all others bring data."

Measurement is the key to understanding that all strategy navigation is on track to the vision and that milestones are reached. Static measures are vital, but indication of direction through performance trends can give views to the consistency and the constancy of performance towards the vision. This may need several tracking charts because the vision is not comprised of one simple goal but can be very complex, with structures dependent on the vision and the type organisation.

Measurement is not enough without responsibility and accountability for teams and individuals. This should be an exciting and supportive process well communicated across the organisation and to all relevant stakeholders, considering confidential and legal obligations.

Budget processes need to create a road map, achieving any budget should be regarded as minimum performance, and all performance should be mapped against key performance and aspirational goals to avoid any false ceiling regarding what could be achieved rather than what cannot. Many times the budget is considered as the aspirational goals that are being asked of performance. This is merely top-line and profit orientation rather than the deeper appreciation that it is requirement based on the organisational resource requirements and is satisfactory performance, albeit based on a static budget that could be outside the current context. It is a base for understanding the construction and cost of the organisation, where additional resources can be applied or adjusted based on any variation with the budget.

SPECIALIST
MANAGEMENT ROLES

T HESE ROLES ARE USUALLY close to the leader and regarded as direct and support roles to the organisation and its stakeholders. There are many others depending on the type of organisation, but these are the few with which I have strong association.

MARKETING

Marketing in and for an organisation is vital. A very short explanation of it is increased profits (achievement of the organisations objectives) through increased customer satisfaction. It's a very skilled area for managing and developing communication, and it needs to support the leader to ensure that the strategic messages are delivered in the best way, at the right time, and to the right audiences. Marketing strategy is a leading element in bringing together the organisation, the leader, and those that the organisation is meant to serve and benefit from. Overarching marketing disciplines are often overlooked as key leadership skills, with senior leaders relying on the marketing specialist or department for support and developing articulations of the pathways to the vision. I am suggesting that leaders need to have an appreciation of marketing and ensure that the marketing team is aligned and supportive of the leadership aspirations.

Very senior leaders are often closely supported by a senior finance executive. Although this is very important from an external view on good governance and financial reporting, marketing needs to play a much stronger internal support to the leadership strategy and its execution. This area of leadership discussion may start to place as much emphasis on the execution to the vision rather than its conception and to-date performance.

The marketing communication strategy has usually had its emphasis on the external customers rather than those who are charged with delivering the customer experience. The tailoring of the customer-orientated message to its specific audiences applies to the internal audience as well. In all promotional programs that I developed, I always considered the internal audience as well as the external (i.e., customers).

The new communication media of electronic and social media require specialised management and specific strategy, and it needs to be conscious in the leader's strategic reviews and adjustments to it because both good and unwelcome news can quickly impact the brand and the feelings (culture) within the businesshood.

The crucial point here is that for the health of the businesshood and its continuing success, the leader needs to have the best and most appropriate, consistent, and constant communication strategy to maintain dominant leadership over the direction and performance of the organisation. Effective communication requires great clarity, and marketing and finance disciplines are required to have clear and concise messages to all necessary audiences. Clarity of the performance is required to drive belief and trust that the strategy and its performance are on track to achieve the objectives and the vision.

Matrix management styles of multiple reporting up and down and across the hood requires progressive performance and its clear communication, with the emphasis being on the performance rather than the delivery of prominent aspects of communication. This requires selfless, egoless leadership and support from all contributors to the strategy.

People will morph in and out of teams as required with the right passionate leadership of this movement. The leader may not be aware of this, and the sub-leaders who also may not be aware. This is where the communication must reach the personnel movements with the reporting systems to communicate performance and feedback on the hood's execution. These sub teams are like the changing subcultures that are circumstantial and can be political by nature—and therefore beneficial or destructive.

The diversity and the dynamic environment that presents in the culture are exacerbated by emotion as well as by having managers with the required skills. They require high emotional intelligence to navigate such a treacherous environment while staying on point.

Marketing's role in successful leadership regimes is paramount with all its creativity and communication tools through its many forms and media. Marketing and the human resource teams need to prepare communication strategies and schedules promoting the organisational goals and leadership directions to the various audiences, supporting the leader in navigating through all the differing courses that, with synchronicity, hopefully lead towards the vision, calling out the milestones along the way. It is vital that all successes at all levels are celebrated to give substance and verification for the direction that the organisation is heading.

In the statement "It was five against five hundred, but I didn't care because I was part of the five hundred," the marketing strategy needs to solicit support from all stakeholders and manage any setbacks that are more than likely inevitable. The best way to manage any political unrest is to have the majority with you even though you may have the power for the moment. The political policy to employ is to have this support from teams, customer frequency, community, media, and stakeholders. Beware of perceptions, no matter where they come from, they are beliefs akin to facts until disputed. These can become very entrenched and difficult to dispute, regardless of the facts. It may require strong, fact-based, presented evidence and potent communication to shift the view. When this happens, it needs to be treated as a fail, and a mistake must be acknowledged, fixed, and learned from. There needs to have been a gap or oversight for this to have happened with information management and communication programs.

FINANCE

MANAGING CAPITAL RESOURCES IS of course a position of power. "He who has the gold has the power," and the leader needs to ensure that resource is where the strategy requires it. Managing information and budgets can manipulate the direction of strategy, and those needs to align with the strategy. A strong professional position, which has a leadership role and a conscience for the business in managing finance and governance, is required for reporting to the regulators and investors while providing management of the capital resource.

It's a very senior, focused role that can be abused by its enthusiasm to control not only the finances but also the leading of the budget process to influence outcomes that may not align with the strategy or the functional capacity, which should be driven by the responsible specialist mangers or teams under the leader's mantle with support from functional specialists. This role can be strategic (i.e., future orientated) but often reacts to what has been achieved, and therefore it is important that the leader communicate the organisation's position and results with an understanding of all the inputs that are in place.

This concern also applies to other influential specialists or strong characters that can mislead the organisation regardless of their intentions. All areas of the organisation need to come together in collaboration and in rhythm to achieve synchronicity.

There is always a need for additional resources and capital, and this can give the finance department leverage (albeit political), or they may be unfairly ridiculed for the way the resource is made available and for the way that financial measures are communicated and dispersed. Again, the leader is accountable to all of this.

SALES MANAGEMENT

I F YOU THINK THAT your organisation is not involved in sales, you must be living under a rock! The sales ethos and effort is right in the middle of everything, and it's everywhere in your organisation's systems and processes. In bringing home the bacon (orders), sales can be singularly given the credit without recognising the organisation and its supporting systems that enabled and fulfilled the sales process. The sales team needs to have a hunger for support in every endeavour for its efficiency and effectiveness because all efficiency is passed down to customers as excellent customer service and fulfilment.

There can be a lot of envy and resentment towards the sales team for the glamour of their role, with client dinners, attending outside-the-organisation events, and their visual presence in the organisation and its wider community. This can lead to an area of conflict and breakdown in the organisation's efficiency and culture, and it's something that leaders need to address. Recognition across all areas of the organisation without favour to any functional team is required for the cross-collaboration and support that builds high-performance organisations. Nevertheless, high achievement needs to be recognised and rewarded. There should always be opportunity and access for all team members to excel and be highly regarded and rewarded.

Of course, leadership attention itself is a scarce resource, and the leader will need to assess and manage time and effort to those areas that require additional support and resources in order to achieve the march towards the vision. The leader will build the executive team and change it as these needs are actioned. The leader, being responsible and accountable for the management of resources, will have a direct impact on the make-up and management of the sales force.

The new, emerging paradigm of digital sales compared to the face-to-face selling systems are creating new selling processes and problems for leaders. The sales people compete with and use these new systems to achieve their sales targets, and the digital and tech-savvy sales teams in the organisation will gain higher competing and achievement profiles. As marketers manage their marketing mix, sales management leaders will need to manage the sales force mix as traditional and virtual channels coexist and operate in parallel to the same customer at times. As in any case, the wider sales scope will challenge the management leadership on supporting diverse channels.

Sales managers can take on a very high profile in an organisation, particularly when it is successful in reporting and managing results and their dissemination. Sometimes they can be responsible for the manipulation of information or results. The leader needs to be confident in the integrity of the organisation's management information systems, knowing that they are communicated correctly and ethically.

The very nature and persuasive skills of the sales managers will have them selling their views and needs to the leader. The leader needs to be cognisant of this, as is the case with any senior manager who is competing for resources or personal recognition.

INFORMATION AND TECHNOLOGY

NFORMATION AND TECHNOLOGY HAS a fantastic opportunity to support communication, simplify the organisation's environment, and provide intelligent information and systems that support the strategy and productivity of the organisation. Technology is evolving and tailored to order at a cost and lifecycle for both software and hardware, and it can be considered a friend or a foe if it is not designed and developed to be consistent, with the strategy being beneficial and useful to all relevant stakeholders. The IT strategy should have a mandate to grow and enable the interface with all beneficiaries, particularly with customers. Often the directive is to cut costs through reducing people rather than growth and improved customer advocacy. Communication and clarity of performance indices is critical for greater involvement and connection with the strategy.

Innovation can be a strong complementing advantage, remembering that innovation is not invention but new application. This is certainly a strong consideration for the leader for efficient and productive progression to the vision.

In terms of simplification, how can the road to the ever-moving vision become shorter to each milestone and easier to reach? The IT department can be a great asset in presenting and coordinating information rather than reams of numbers on reports when graphical desktops can provide direction and excitement in showing progress in real time. This is where a leader needs to have eyes on the world for new developments that can be helpful to the organisation.

Technology drives are often focused on lowering costs and labour heads, but a key component of success should include growth and, with a growing workforce, a more efficient, bigger market penetration.

With the ever-expanding collection of data and its transfer into meaningful information and the excitement surrounding the digital world of communication, the effort can be applied to the buzz of it all, rather than the key focus for the leader being its application to the strategy. The focus for the leader is greater connectivity strategies for integration and collaborations of systems for reducing costs, as well as bringing together and sourcing the beneficiaries that are integral for performance and reaching the vision. The networks that traditionally occupied leaders over dinners and gala events are now available in the virtual world as well. Connectivity of shareholders and owners, suppliers, and customers' needs to be a prime advocacy, and the leader and the team will have strategies for securing them and maintaining loyalty. The virtual and real networks and their timely connectivity make a larger hood that can be more complex or beneficial at a cost-effective, global scale.

The leader has a new paradigm to work through to use the IT teams as strategic elements to achieve performance rather than enabling and data gathering to score the performance and governance standards.

There is a lot of glitter and hype in the IT world, and keeping programs relevant and meaningful to the customer base is paramount. A good case is with some banking organisations moving away from face-to-face customer contact and losing trust. They are now trying to find the right balance of IT efficiency against customer relationships. Be aware of form over function. Keep in mind that nothing happens without people being involved.

SUPPORT EXECUTIVE

UPPORT EXECUTIVES ON SUCH teams as legal, corporate executive, human resource, and boards have key roles, and their involvement can impact the direction and strategy. Such needs must be kept in balance with the capability and capacity of the organisation. Being bound by rules and laws without challenge can lead to cannot rather than can-do organisations. I am not suggesting that leaders don't follow laws, but their critical thinking needs to challenge how they operate within them. As the saying goes, there is more than one way to skin a cat. In some cases, less is more. Remember the principle of keeping the operating environment simple.

From the above, you can quickly recognise the dilemma for the leader to manage the assorted styles and the individual within the executive roles that can impact on the leadership's direction. The leader needs to ensure that all the executives have the necessary resources and scope of control to achieve their roles and specific objectives, and that they also complement within the organisation and the overall strategy. In many cases, this is the group that controls political unrest and may have designs on the leader's role or a separate, unaligned view on the vision or strategy. The leader has a direct responsibility to be decisive and action-orientated to correct any unaligned activity.

The above are internal issues, and the external issues are also under the leader's scope of influence and decision-making. Decision-making for a leader is rarely a yes or no process; it is more about how the decision impacts the health of the organisation and supports the team's progress to achieve the vision within its current context. The leader sets the frequency or parameters of scope for each department, and the key is for executives to ensure parts of the strategy and delivery of success factors as teams and individuals (sub-leaders) achieve objectives. Strategic plans are vital, but decisive action is required, and decision-making must take place within the frequency ranges set by the leader because no organisation or business can be all things to all people. I have often referred to the quote "Narrow your focus and increase your lead."

Primary drivers and influencers are about power and contribution, and they usually have a gain to be had out of the organisation's substance. There are intents in their decision-making and the leader needs to ensure that the organisation is competitive or popular for contribution in achieving the traction for the strategic progress towards the vision.

The issue with taking counsel from highly specialist individuals is that the information comes with a specialised bias and individual intent with their consideration.

BOARDS

BOARDS HAVE A RESPONSIBILITY to their shareholders and the type of leadership that will achieve the vision. In such cases, the board will choose the leader and have a view on its vision and how the organisation is to run. It will have an overseeing role in terms of governance and performance timelines. The leader will need to sell the vision and the strategy to the board and then pass it down the channel of contributors. This leads to the question of who devises the strategy, who accepts it, and who executes and continues to challenge the separation of leadership from management. The leader needs to recognise the bias in the board's decisions and then sell the strategy to gain their support, keeping in mind that they have hire and fire power over the leader. This highlights the fact in culture that there are subsets of vision that the leader must integrate into strategy to achieve their primary vision.

CUSTOMERS

THE VERY EXISTENCE OF an organisation is to service customers, accepting that this may be a specific target group that can satisfy the financial requirements and vision for the business. The leader's role is to define the customer's segments that the business is targeting and requires in satisfying its performance requirements, which are typically financial.

Having a culture that is customer biased is a cornerstone towards a strategically holistic, human-faced, performance organisation. Nothing happens without people, and any opportunity to engage across the hood with a customer value–based behaviour will deliver rewards. Customers are now able to engage from afar and have greater choices, and as the hood strives to become the employer of choice, it must be the first choice for customers, whether face-to-face or virtual.

SUPPLIERS

S UPPLIERS ARE OFTEN AN untapped resource. A businesses supplier can have so much to offer because its success is linked to the hood's customers. This is where there can be strong allegiances of leaders and their complementing strategies, sharing of resources and processes to successfully satisfy all strategies as independent and shared milestones are met along the journey towards consistent and constant customer satisfaction.

The leader needs to look outside the organisation and source the key suppliers, whose success (or not) wash across their organisation, promoting its ability to achieve its goals. Also give consideration for emerging newer, innovative suppliers and stakeholders who may be needed for consideration as additional or replacement suppliers.

The leader's role and presence needs to align all these influences on the strategy and its vision, bringing them into a synchronicity that has a smooth progress towards excellence in achieving the vision. Judgement and assessment need to be based on performance and how it is delivered. The inputs should align to deliver the desired output and outcome. Too many scorecards are focused on measuring outputs only, without giving exposure and recognition to the inputs that are critical for the delivery of robust outputs.

MARKETING

ARKETING AND COMMUNICATION IS the essence of influence and gaining alignment across the organisation to achieve directed synchronicity from all groups. If you don't have an appreciation of marketing and its audiences, you will more than likely have shortcomings in selling the strategic direction for the vision and gaining deep belief for it throughout the organisation. In most marketing exercises, a program will require approaches that cater to internal and external markets, including supply chain stakeholders and all beneficiaries.

In selling the vision and executing strategy, it needs to be succinct, targeted, and defined in methods that all the various audiences can understand. Any pictorial enhancement is usually of great benefit but needs to be clear on milestones and timings.

The creative needs to be carried forward in reporting and feedback loops. Marketing managers often refer to the consistency of the messages to aid recall, but the other key C is constancy. The constant presentation and delivery of the message is vital to refresh, reinforce, and update positions.

A great amount of any organisation's resources and effort is put to its marketing program. The marketing executive should have a key role in developing the communication strategy to sell the vision and the strategy because he or she has the skills and creative resources. The leader should use the marketing skills and all others to ensure that the vision and its strategy are sold and that its progress is well reported. Marketing ideology (i.e., customer-focused) that sees all stakeholders as customers should be prominent not only in crafting the strategy but also in its implementation.

In many organisations, this can be left to the operational executive and sales teams, which can be quite forceful in execution by the very nature of their daily activities and routines. Creating excitement can seem simple but is often overlooked in presenting business plans that are necessary, but it can be boring to the general audience. The communication and the essence of the plan should be an exciting exercise and is very motivating.

Communication is a dynamic and should be a continuing conversation with the audience. Testing its understanding and adjusting to it is a continuous exercise. In any misunderstanding, with its retransmission, the leader needs to be aware of and adjust to any propaganda that may have been distributed. Any follow-up designed for clarifying or counteracting the original message, or for some political motivation, will create some confusion. Communication is getting the message across, but the leader will be more interested in the action that it creates and the relevant outcomes. Marketing managers are disciplined and stay on the formal message, but they need to manage the informal communication that is a result of unaligned culture or individuals. Source is a very strong influencer on the credibility of the message, and the leader must own this. Any unaligned communiqués and the noise that is created by all media should be dealt with and then have it redirected back to plan. Once communication hits the wider audience, the media are out of the control of the communication strategist.

With such diversity in organisations, one communication strategy is not enough. The uptake and its further communication will be impacted by timings and understanding, and there may be some misconstruing, whether intentional or not. Leaders need to have ears at the base of the organisation, understand the informal communication, and rescript and remarket the message as required.

The organisation is all about people, and the performance is delivered by them, not systems or machines or digital devices. The marketing ethos is about delivering information through various communication media to people, no matter how we categorise them (customers, employees, team members, etc.). In supporting all these groups, the leader needs to understand where they are at with the strategy and their understanding of the performance and vision for the organisation.

The basis of marketing is often referred to as the 4 Ps, which are Porter's 4 pillars for marketing strategy. But with marketing as a strategic function for leadership, I have 6Ps that all leaders and marketers supporting the leader should consider. Their communication issues are broader, whereas the marketing function on its own is centred on customer engagement. With leadership, the communication strategy has a wider customer base to influence.

The diverse media for communication require the 6 Ps for discussion on modern marketing communication. It is worth noting that the modern marketing challenges have to do with communication to people, dealing with information, and the perception of the organisation or brand. The 6 Ps in this discussion focus on what a leader should be concentrating on for achievement of the broader strategy, rather than focussing on strategic marketing. For an organisation to move forward, it must be done with and through people and communication. This is paramount for leading them in the right direction. Many a leader and manager love their high-level presentations, and this is gratifying to their own egos. However, getting the message communicated is one thing, and having the messages enacted is another. This is where highly successful leaders and managers get going down on the ground, so to speak, making sure that communication is clear and uncluttered. Any misunderstanding is to be dealt with, and any conflict or resistance is managed openly and with respect. While the people concerned are on the team, they are important to its overall success. There will be unpleasant issues that may be underlying, and these need to be raised to the surface by putting the dead cat (issue) on the table, announcing that the cat is dead, and taking the issue onboard if it cannot be solved directly. Recognise that the cat is dead. It is very important to call out what is wrong and then deal with it.

Deal with people—or should I say, team members who are negative, are resisting, or do not understand—upfront if they don't understand what is required of them. In dealing with aggression or enthusiastic resistance, I have coined the love technique. In simple terms, it means being reassuring, positive, and supportive but staying on mission. People with this trait have an expectation to be met aggressively, and the love technique floors them. You can have the positive upper hand very quickly. In a physical sense, it is getting them to understand that you are on their side while they are on the team, and they remain on the team while they add value and contribute to the vision.

Communication is a two-way street and is a web of information and misinformation, with noise and interference through which the leader must find pathways. The main point is in communicating that the message has been successfully received, let alone acted upon. It will require mass, targeted programs, and any opportunity for face-to-face communication should be embraced. This gives an opportunity to feel if there is any informal communication that needs to be dealt with, or if a change of message is required. The leader should test every level of understanding for what is to be done, and he or she should measure and report on progress.

Too much effort is put into how we communicate and how much, rather than what we communicate and why. If communication is not achieving its objectives, then as with any issue, you need to revisit the source and the construction of the message. The source is where communication most often fails.

THE 6 PS: MARKETING IN LEADERSHIP

1. PEOPLE

I NDIVIDUALS CAN HAVE SUCH an impact with so many roles and views in their relationship with the businesshood: employee, customer, shareholder, political inclinations, cultural strengths, religious views, and a stakeholder in the hood, to call out a few. Teams, audiences, and their media are a new, complicated issue for the leader in strategizing the communication mix. I worked for Goodyear Tyre and Rubber Australia for many years, and I always carried with me one of their mantras: "Goodyear people make the difference." Never lose sight that nothing happens without people, even in this digital age. Marketing is all about bringing products and services to satisfy customers, and the strategy should define the required number of customers to satisfy the business's financial and strategic requirements. No matter how targeted a message is designed to be, it will reach a wider range of people. and this could lead to misunderstanding and conflict to the brand position and subsequently the organisation's image.

Communication therefore needs to be concise and factual, with little room for misinterpretation. People can also be very supportive of an organisation that has been historically well received by all stakeholders, and this is where the strategy for the businesshood must be supported and understood by the marketing team. All marketing messages are aligned with the leader's strategy to provide a synergistic movement for the achievement of its vision. The hood is a team which will consist of subcultures and various tribes that will naturally want to achieve its so-called vision. The leader needs to understand the dynamics within these teams and appreciate that they lead people individually and as groups.

2. PERSONABLE

Like brands, leaders need to be believable and give the impression that they're approachable for people to align their own values and give support to. Modern communication media have messages delivered directly, are immediate in their response and feedback from all recipients at all stakeholder levels, and are timely and far-reaching as well. The messages quickly become a developing story with many authors with different perceptions and agendas, and the leader or marketing manager needs to be on song and continue to address the veracity and direction of these messages with continued, constant adjustments with strategic change and managing, reacting to the many various perceptions of the messages.

The key for leaders and brand management is constancy for reinforcing the strategic direction and the brand's management. Being consistent is not enough because the businesshood is under review, growth, and attack from outside and within, whether formally or informally. Reviews and challenges to the current view at every opportunity is the new digital way based on truth, misunderstanding, or politically driven views at odds with the leader's and the hood's strategy.

Social networks have a direct connection to individuals at the same time as the masses and make it more difficult to control information as fact and within context. The businesshood needs to be managed more like a brand, with the leader being the conductor of all the teams and stakeholders, managing and delivering information.

Communication needs to be crafted so that it is understood and meaningful to the individual rather than being theatrical or award-winning. The individual can comment to the world using social media and therefore become an advocate or a problematic adversary. Marketers often rely on research which historically is collected as factors of thought, beliefs, and opinions. In being personable, decision makers should find every opportunity to listen directly to their constituents and customers alike by collecting verbatim comments for wider review and action. A verbatim review can remove any bias, but also be aware that they need to be reoccurring. "One swallow does not make a spring." Also, beliefs are not always fact but can be communicated as such.

The digital world has made it fast and furious in collecting and disseminating information, and we need to have objective marketers and managers that are able to collect, rationalise, disseminate, and change quickly to address whatever is required. It should also have an intuition as to what is real and relevant, and stay close with the leader's evolving strategy and direction.

One voice in today's world has a wide, active audience that can work for you or against you, whether it is an internal or external circumstance. Deployment of the marketing effort needs to be efficient, but it needs to be mindful in its design that the individual, whether part of the targeted audience or not, will be an adversary or advocate. In reflecting on being personable, we all need to place greater value on every member of the team, and the importance and value of every customer and stakeholder who takes the time to express a view on the organisations performance.

The best way for the leader to be personable is to be available, and the digital environment can be an efficient medium to enable the early explanation for what is not understood, filtering commentary and counteracting any non-factual communication.

The digital approach is most efficient, but the most effective is the old-fashioned management approach of walking around the organisation and at the very least being seen.

The marketing message is designed for action, and as such, action can only happen through people (individuals and teams). Management theory deals with spans of influence and control, and although the new digital media are efficient with reach, we need to ensure that it not just an easy practice but remains warm and reflective. It is very prominent in this discussion that the leader and marketing resources need to operate on the strategy constantly.

3. PRAGMATIC

Integrity and values deal with facts. Reporting on all aspects of the business in a simple and clear method creates a competitive and involved environment for the teams to continue to improve. This requires highlighting and reporting on the key performance indicators for the hood's health. The issue with this reporting is that it is in the present, which does not give an indication as to where they are heading to achieve future goals.

The other important aspect in reporting information and performance is accountability. I strongly support the identification of the primary team members or teams that are responsible for the performance that is being reported. Keeping an elevated level of transparency brings trust and attracts team members who want to be a member of a high-performance team without any hidden political bias. In being pragmatic and fact-seeking, leaders need to also be open to subjective views and assessments of any aspect that leads to supporting or developing the strategy.

Facts can be presented in softer formats than pages of figures with charts and graphs which can be better understood by many and then supported, rather than feeling threatened by masses of figures. There has been a move towards more engaging dashboards that not only highlight current performance but also give an indication for their likely trend.

Transparency and availability is a keystone to establishing trust in the organisation's performance and the strategy's worth. Although there are elements that are confidential and sensitive, this is accepted and taken as normal practice.

Also in the context of being pragmatic is staying the course and when the facts dictate changing course or strategy as required. Staying down to earth and being fact-driven does not mean being insensitive. It requires the ability to see the forest for the trees without losing the detail in showing the bigger picture and keeping in mind the audience.

4. PURPOSEFUL

Why does the organisation exist, and why does it need a leader? All communication needs to have purpose and be meaningful to those who are exposed to it. There needs to be greater benefits to the individual other than extrinsic rewards, and there is nothing more gratifying than having a valued purpose and contribution for the use of one's time and being recognised for such contribution, particularly amongst peers and the community (hood). To achieve the vision, an organisation will need to have many purposes for its achievement. Achieving these goals is one thing, but it is also the timing of the execution and recognising the achievement that is important. Creating an understanding across the teams of where and what their purposes are delivers an opportunity to collaborate with others, bringing about a synergy that delivers a synchronicity within the organisation whereby things just seem to happen. This is a very great outcome, and its significance should not be overlooked. In the achievement of one goal, there may be many purposes for its overarching achievement: financial gain, environmental improvement, better OH&S outcomes, and benefits to the community.

5. PUBLIC (COMMUNITY RESPONSIBILITY)

The very fabric of the businesshood is where it fits, benefits, and contributes in the community regarding its direct relationship and virtual neighbourhood (network) that it contributes to and gains insight, inspiration, and value from. To be sustainable, it must contribute as well as draw resources from the hood and grow. Being visible either by location or branding brings great accountability, and the leader needs to understand and contribute to the community with leadership and resources, as well as being a responsible member of the community, whether by charitable or behavioural means, in its approach to the environment and community. Leaders assess their organisation to mitigate risk, and they can bring this expertise to a community level as well (i.e., into the homes of their team members or the wider community) through ensuring that their organisation is a righteous example. This can be as little as making sure any communication is consistent with such an approach. When we discuss a learning organisation, we can tend to overlook the simple learnings that have greater beneficial reach as well, as in the case with greater safety awareness and process for mitigating risk.

In being a professional example, the leader and the organisation will have a high regard within the community, and there will be benefits that are returned to the organisation in favour through customer loyalty and support with increased patronage.

Any organisation is a group of people, and groups have power and influence. This influence can be at a political level, or the personal growth of individuals within an organisation can have a powerful contribution to the wider community. The power of one times one should not be overlooked because this is people power at its best.

6. PERFORMANCE

To know where you are going, you need to understand where you are at and where you have been. This applies to all who have a stake or are contributors. In noting this, it is all about the optimum transparent information and reporting systems that are prudent and practical.

Not all members need to have a detailed report or understanding of the organisation's performance. They will have trust if they are given an indication of progress and trends predicting where they will be and how their performances impact the organisation.

Performance is a jigsaw of contribution that needs to be timely and recognisable in blending the organisation's performance to the achievement of its goals and vision.

The challenge for a leader is to achieve current performance and develop a process for measuring and guiding future performance. Such a process is more than creating a five- or ten-year budget. It's bringing such a visionary outlook into the psyche of the hood. This also delivers a strong message that the organisation is strong and confident, and there's an opportunity for all to grow in the hood.

As in decision-making, breaking down performance criteria in smaller pieces and giving these as key performance targets for teams and individuals is a powerful way to unleash contribution and create the synchronicity that is evident in high-performing organisations.

BRANDS AND THE
POWER OF SYMBOLS

B RANDS AND SYMBOLS ARE so important and influential in disseminating powerful feelings of trust, belief, and connection with a mission and its position within the hood. Organisations are continually in a state of change, and business symbols and brands can give continuity over extended periods of time (and changes of leadership). As we move further into the digital age, it is becoming more reliant on images and symbols to give brevity to communication and have greater reach in the understanding of what is being communicated and in what context. The point here is that audiences are becoming broader, with greater levels of comprehension and their own beliefs. The further the reach, the greater the opportunity for feedback—and vandalism to the brand and its messages.

Marketing managers and leaders will need to be ahead of this and move more into marketing leadership rather than simply marketing management or internal leadership. This will require taking the high ground with all communication in creating brands that have such integrity that they can withstand the vandalism that can occur through the electronic communication channels. Even when the message may not be a great or positive one, it is better to control it rather than have to react in unfavourable and militant contexts.

When building a brand proposition, it is vital that it meets the needs of the vision and the purpose of the organisation in taking a broad definition of customers' needs. The brand's internal and external messages should reflect the acquisition and building of their loyalty as key.

Symbolism and crafted messages can build a dynamic following, but consistency and constancy of the proposition and its position builds a history that creates memorable brands and loyalty, which creates brand advocates.

No matter how intelligent the specialists are who create the brand with all its creativity and style, it is subject to perception change because there are external changes such as fashion that reflect on every communication that is broadcast. The leader is responsible for and accountable to its impact and the strategy for dealing with its management.

LEADERSHIP
CONSIDERATIONS

TEAMS

S O MUCH EMPHASIS IS placed on team performance, but often it is only a few individuals within a team who generate exceptional performance. A team's functional area or a division's performance is reported by the business information systems, but it does not point out the inputs or individuals that are generating such performance. There is often talk of high-performance teams, and there seems to be some political correctness with this because it is the leaders of these teams who are more often given credit for generating success and are consequently rewarded. This supports the executive team structure and its standing as a group of high achievers, but it can generate a type of groupthink or protected society. There may be times when the leader of the team does not necessarily have to be at the lead of the team for that level of performance. This is often evident when the leader is under skilled or is politically savvy to take advantage of the individual or groups of high performers within the team.

Leaders need to ensure that recognition and reward is given to the individual as well when the team is given such accolades. By protecting their team or themselves by not recognising individual performance, leaders can bring about defection from their team. This is very evident within teams with high turnover and variable performances within the organisation. Leadership can be delivered in many ways, and the leader may be perceived to be leading by not leading an exercise or project.

The other side of the coin is that leaders put their efforts towards what is not working, and the managers of these teams are given greater exposure. This can be seen to be a reward for mediocre or lacklustre performance. The more time, effort, or resource a leader puts into these situations, the more it can become a greater drain on resources and an impasse. They are likely to gild the lily through subsidised resource or propaganda-driven pretence. This can become a snowballing effect as team leaders compete for resources and the attention of the leader, which is a very scarce resource itself. They may be misdirected to improving deficient performance areas rather than dealing with their own leadership issues and the real level of performances at hand in the division.

Teams are a great resource for information but are often overlooked. I can understand that it may be difficult to ascertain truth because the team has is its own cultural and political systems. As is the case with many whistle-blowers, any derogative commentary can be disastrous to an aspiring individual or team who brings information to the leader's desk that may be contrary to that which has been delivered by the direct team leader or is calling out cultural, legal or strategy misbehaviours. It's a very delicate area, and organisations need to have a strong set of organisational values in place.

In truly understanding team performance, you must be able to recognise and measure individual performances as well. Teams are a product of individuals.

SPIRIT

The leader has the responsibility of being the conscience of the organisation and the energiser for ensuring that there is a great spirit amongst the teams. Wherever there is competition and gain, there will always be a temptation for personal benefit. The leader needs to instil an integrity and morality that is more than an expectation. It is a simple chronicle and example of how things are done and how they are called out and dealt with when both good and bad behaviour occurs.

There will also be times when the businesshood's communities require support from the organisation. This can be from disaster support to supporting arm's-length opportunities and charities that do not directly support the organisation. These actions should be a result of how the organisation sees its responsibilities within the businesshood, and not merely a strategic reaction to enhance reputation and brand presence. Although the leader is the custodian of the brand and the business's reputation, the hood and its cultural behaviours within and without the organisation will also impact wider spheres and future opportunities.

The spirit of the organisation needs to be generational in that it inspires future members to accept dramatic leadership changes that can happen very unexpectedly. The spirit of the organisation needs to lift and be ongoing when it is needed.

The businesshood is all about people, and they will make the difference whatever that is. They need to be prepared by the leader for whatever may eventuate in such a wide-reaching community of people with common and uncommon purpose and differing goals while living and operating in their common benefiting hoods.

High spirits deliver so much energy and focus and usually arise out of a well-led culture with focus and benefit available for all.

PEOPLE

People make the difference, and this can cut both ways as far as performance and strategy go. The leader needs to ensure that the people are right for their roles and teams, and that the executive team is appropriate for the challenges at hand and can adapt to future challenges. This may require changes to the team members as the businesshood stays on its strategic course.

Leadership is stewardship. No leader will last forever and therefore has a responsibility to develop and improve the teams while planning his or her own succession and that of the teams.

Again, it needs to be said that individuals make up teams. Where appropriate, they need to be recognised and rewarded as individuals.

Leaders have tough roles at times, and their decisions can impact people deeply. Such actions go with the leadership role, but leaders should never lose sight of humanity and their responsibilities in leading the hood.

Human resources have a huge responsibility to develop and hone the skills of the team for optimising the capability and performances aligned to the strategy and the business's goals. The HR department needs to stay disciplined because it does not need to involve itself in the operational management of the business. There is a failing within human resource departments to push into policing roles rather than the strategic development of the people power within the organisation and developing the longevity of the business through succession and updating skills with education and technology. This is another example of the requirement of sub strategy and sub vision needing to complement the master vision, and of the organisation having the ability to embrace and adapt to change.

The human resource function needs to be much more visionary, with its operational purpose on improving capability and capacity with training, talent identification programs, and development pathways through the organisation. On a more strategic level, what are the horizons that need to be met with digital technology and faster communication streams? With so much occurring in our world, it is a wonder and a travesty that we spend less time developing people than we do developing the digital systems. The decision makers and leaders of tomorrow will still be people, and they will need people of a certain mettle and with developed skills to support them in achieving futuristic visions.

As I have mentioned, morale is vital for progressive change, and human resource programs need to be cognisant of this and be active in ensuring its health. I have witnessed a human resource department so tied up with imposed and self-made bureaucracy that it lost sight of the human resources it was meant to be developing and supporting. It spent more resources on scoring turnover than understanding its cause, and hence it was unable to address the human hole in the organisation.

CONTEXT

Leadership is all about moving people, whether by guiding or providing the appropriate resources for them to excel and contribute to the business goals. The leader should provide the easiest and most appropriate route through a strategy and then develop a team that works within the context of the current organisational structure, market environment, and the organisation's current capabilities and capacity.

Context is complex because it can be more perception or mere confusion as an aggregate of unaligned perceptions. It is incumbent on the leader to understand what it is and what needs to be done to align, and to construct the required context to the strategy. Often discussion is on the learning organisation when dealing with what such a complexity requires. This requires that the leader needs to be a learning leader as well as lead a learning organisation. This can be put in simple terms, such as continuous improvement programs and by personal example.

The strongest element of context is belief, and once achieved, it accelerates alignment and velocity to the strategy and its vision.

The context is almost the framework which supports the culture and its management. It is very relevant because it provides the day-to-day operation, structure, and relevance for the organisation rather than generalisations that are about personal specialisations and capability. Transparency of progress and recognition for achievement to strategic milestones is important for the morale and consistency of progress for the organisation. The other important aspect of context is that it is also dynamic and needs to adapt for external changes and managed, based on the need for internal changes and changes to strategy at diverse levels of progress to the developing vision. Often there has been textbook talk about a learning organisation, and it is vital that the leader ensures that the people are developing in skill and understanding to manage the forced and required contextual changes. The leader should also ensure that the organisation is learning in process changes that allow and encourage the organisation to evolve.

This approach should seek such learning from where it can. It should not overlook the wisdom and experience that exists throughout the organisation while encouraging innovation.

When strategically looking at context, we should ensure that the organisation is capable within its current context and is ready for the future challenges. This will require very strong leadership to navigate through the difficult contextual challenges, and leaders need to have the courage to innovate and lead a strategic vision.

LEADERSHIP
APPLICATION

I HAVE OFTEN BEEN ASKED, "What is leadership, and how do I become a better leader?" Such a question is an indication of having some leadership traits. The one point that is in every discussion on leadership is vision. A leader wants to change or move the hood into a new context and performance. I have often responded in simple terms that it is about moving a hood in a desired direction. In movement, it can be a simple program (i.e., transition) to a new operating system, or it can be a complete change in business strategy with a new, refreshed vision.

In developing your own approach, you may consider the 10 Ps of instituting your own leadership.

10 PS OF INSTITUTING LEADERSHIP

1. PEOPLE. Having the right informed people involved with both skills and team fit is vital. "A team of champions will always be beaten by a champion team." A leader doesn't lead anything but people and subsequently teams. There is extreme complexity in leading and managing people and teams. Teams are comprised of individuals, and the astute leader will keep the operating and strategy elements of their direction simple and the communication succinct, with plenty of opportunity to provide recognition. One

of the issues is how to stretch people and teams without losing the realism of believing in what can be achieved. Big, hairy, audacious goals without milestones to reach them might seem too far out of reach. They need to be broken down to smaller, relevant, and more timely achievements and then assigned across the hood. If anyone is to put limits on people, let it be themselves. They and the leader will be amazed at what they are capable of with the right encouragement and support. Externally, leaders should also be very close to their customers, who are beneficiaries of the organisation's products or services.

2. PURPOSE. Do not overlook the power of having a powerful common purpose that not only focuses the teams but also has a collaborating effect within the culture. Cultures in organisation are often defined as the sum of behaviours. Having purpose gives structured reasoning and energy for achieving the organisation's goals. It goes further than extrinsic reward and can satisfy the deep emotional, personal drives while crossing over all the functional teams within the organisation.

An organisation with a common purpose also has the opportunity for common benefit in its achievement. This is a reward in itself with all the benefits that are generated by a successful hood.

3. PROCESS is the key to operations, and it should be kept simple. Technology needs to be considered where it can to allow a wider range of people to be involved and contribute to the organisation through the creation of simpler operating environments. Process is meant to simplify and allow for greater involvement, allowing more to be great rather than struggling with bureaucracy and unclear, complex operating programs. This is also critical for the health and safety of people and for having a minimal risk or no-risk environment. Noting the existence of the operating environment leads to strategizing with the people and teams in consideration for its ongoing development. Processes need to be available, well documented, and relevant to those who have access and are involved with their application.

4. POLICY needs to set the required boundaries and set the scope of control for all participants in the system or subsystem. Knowing the scope for a task gives confidence and negates the overpowering bureaucracy that can develop and strangle individual and team contributions, creating confusion and chaos in direction and management control. Again, policy needs to be simply developed and stated, and it should be open to review as change requires. It needs to be accessible, authorised, and in print. Policy needs to be helpful in providing direction rather than a power or control mechanism.

5. PARTICIPATION in every small way, referencing the strategy and the impacts on its achievement, will create greater support and a team approach. It is easy to overlook the third-party influencers on strategy (such as suppliers and financiers) as key stakeholders. All stakeholders need to be considered for collaboration, benefit, and cooperation across all areas that can be involved to improve the strategic context and the organisation's success. Every person who touches the organisation is a participating stakeholder at some level, whether or not one is a direct beneficiary.

6. PROGRESS. As discussed, leadership is all about movement. To manage that, the organisation should progress the correct way with the strategy. The progress needs to be measured and be as widely reported as possible. It may be required to have a few different scorecards that are reported within the various levels of the organisation and the external environment. A scorecard that is overarching of all contributors to the vision is critical to bring together an understanding that roles within an organisation are not competing or merely complementary to others, but are crucial to each other's success. This approach supports the fact that connectivity is not only a virtual and technical reality; it is also an organisational reality. For it to succeed, it needs to connect within itself in every way, indirectly or directly. To understand progress, the leader needs to have measures and communication in place, always referencing the progress towards the vision.

7. PERCEPTION. This may seem a bit abstract at first, but no matter how wrong they are, perceptions can be regarded as fact. This can be an innocent view that gathers momentum, and it can be very difficult and divisionary for the leader to deal with. The leader needs to be proactive with communication, transparency, approachability, and openness in order to ensure that the organisation is perceived in the correct light and that its integrity is upheld. The bigger issue is when misinformation is circulated, and this can be driven from customers, employees, competitors, or media organisations. It is something to closely watch, with the rise of social forums and electronic media. Perception is reality, and the leader must be continually listening to what is a perception, reacting accordingly with fact or parking the issue until it can be dealt with appropriately.

8. POSITION. I have discussed at length the internal issues to which leaders must apply themselves. In thinking about position, the leader needs to have an appreciation as to the organisation's position in the real world with measures such as market share, share price, return on investments, competitive position, brand perception, any critical benchmarking regarding efficiency, and more. This is an area where leaders rely on networking and third-party research for assistance and advice. There is a big issue in understanding the best fit with positions in satisfying all beneficiaries; being too far left or right of strategised position will be at some type of cost or risk. The leader must manage his or her personal position and that of the organisation. The integrity and culture of the organisation is always under review by all stakeholders who invest or continue to benefit. The importance of brand and symbolisation is paramount to a hood's position within wider hoods.

9. PARTICULARS are the specifics of what leaders make decisions upon. In leadership, they are dealing with the realities or facts of a situation. Often the leader will be in a constant state of checking, rechecking, and testing the facts for decision-making purposes. Facts are often twisted in their presented context and by the various agendas that are supported by the presentation of facts. Whatever their delivered purpose, facts are just information, and there is

always plenty of that about. One fact may be at odds with another in aiding the decision process. The leader needs to know where the organisation is at and the next missions to move forward within the leader's resources to keep on course and maintain the desired vision. In dealing with facts and truth, you can declutter and eradicate a lot of the rhetoric that managers tend to try to impress with by having simple metrics for measurement and allowing open review as much as possible.

10. PERFORMANCE, or profit, should not be lost. The very purpose of the organisation is to achieve and evolve the development of team members and improve the culture and community benefit. One measure over another does not excuse poor performance no matter how morally right one may be. I have witnessed well-managed programs in poorly performing organisations. The point is that no matter how well that manager managed, he was still involved with the deficient performance of the hood. The leader's very existence is to achieve the output objectives while implementing and creating the inputs that bring about success. The leader needs to ensure that objectives are aligned to the relevant responsible teams and that progress is timely and readily available in understandable, measurable reports and communications. There are some organisations that purport to being non-profit, but they will have profit-orientated objectives to ensure beneficiaries are catered to and resources are maintained and gained to achieve their vision.

The Ps of implementing leadership direction provide strategic thought to design the simplest operating environment for people to be great and grow in, rather than searching for the greatest individuals for the team. Too often the operational teams are seen to be the leaders rather than the strategic managers in executing the strategy. Although great operators require higher levels of leadership, it is a subset of the organisation and the leader's vision. This attention can draw away from the long-term health of the business because operational management can often have short-term goals that are against the long-term goals related to the vision and strategic leadership. In thinking about the distinct roles within the hood's organisation, it can be confusing as to what and who is important. This can be the case when powerful managers have a greater voice or presence than the organisation's overall position. This confusion can lead to conflict and imbalances within the organisation, putting politicking in front of leadership guidance to the strategy and its progress.

Having a leader means having a desire for a strategically led hood as opposed to the fierce presence of the operating, managed organisation. It is this recognition of the support that leadership brings to all roles in the hood that enables the organisation to be more capable and enduring

TIME

O FTEN THOUGHT ABOUT IN a time-management context, time can be considered almost infinite by applying human resources to gain effectiveness; think about building the pyramids. However, time can also be the scarcest resource of all. Leadership is occupied with how to make the most out of time with all the resources at one's disposal. This is due to having grand visions and acknowledging that one's own time is limited.

How do you create an environment that makes it easier for all to contribute to the organisation's goals? I have mentioned previously that many new leaders to an organisation will obliterate the organisation and its structure and then implement their own ideas, people, and structure without recognising the latent talent value or having a true understanding of what the organisation needs to achieve. There is no doubt that there are some disasters that require an immediate change. However, implementing and starting strategy and human resources again puts a leader well behind any timeline that he may have, and that is huge competitive risk. This is a revolutionary approach, and before razing the organisation and starting again, leaders should look at the value of an evolutionary approach one that is implemented at speed. Setting the right environment (i.e., management context, often referred to as the learning organisation) and winning the team over can be a very strong competitive and adaptive advantage, but it does require time. New leaders will have a firm understanding of the weaknesses of the organisation but, maybe they should also research the weaknesses of the previous leaders and their strategies before implementing their own strategy and vision. The revolutionary approach can make the leader look in charge and control, but it only has a small window before performance and accountability come into question.

Evolution is creating an environment that encourages learning, continuous improvement, and collaboration with the coexistence of departments and divisions, understanding that in such an approach, all are personally benefitted and with recognition and a sense of belonging. It's often coined continuous improvement that is generated and led by individuals and teams. It's not based on survival but on being the best that they can be and achieving high-performance goals and star-struck visions. These teams may not sense the efficiencies of such collaboration, but the synchronicity of their contributions creates rewards that reinforce the behaviours.

In making the most of time, there needs to be a clear direction, and one must apply human and intelligent resources efficiently and effectively. This is often looked at as a cost application and is the subject of business strategy regarding what is the correct financial cost for the application of achievement towards a set of goals in a prescribed period.

We all have time; it's simply a question of what we want to do with it and the opportunity cost of one action over another. The leader has the wonderful resource of people, and when they come together in high-performance teams, they can create world-record achievements within record time and exceed the expectations of their own goals. When people and teams come together seamlessly, there is a synchronicity of achievement created that could be described as exponential effort, and this can be unrecognised because it seems to happen naturally. The effect is phenomenal, but it doesn't happen without strategic, holistic leadership. This comes from great leaders who value great vision and so-called normal people who do wonderful things.

I have included this section on time because upon reflection, a leader will look over her past, and one of the self-critical questions should be how well she used her time and the time of others.

EXECUTION

L EADERSHIP WITH ALL ITS drive, creativity, and vision is fruitless without good executive management. Managers at this level work closely in the continuous development of the vision and its strategy, but they are responsible for the processes and systems that are required to deliver objectives while balancing the capacity and capability of the organisation to deliver strategy within financial and resource constraints. Leadership is not only about delivering aspiration. It is also about giving the confidence, discipline, and intelligence to implement and manage a process while giving permission for improvement within a shared and evolving environment. Therefore the leader is continually developing the system that supports the processes that enable achievement.

Good process management not only ensures quality, guidance, and consistency but also instils trust with all stakeholders, enabling transparency and the efficient and effective management of resources and culture. Without process and rules, there can only be anarchy of effort, which despite any good intentions results in chaos and failure. This leads to misdirection and affects quality at every level and application within the organisation. There is always goodwill within people and teams, but this can be naive and non-systematic in achieving the vision in a synchronistic manner without articulated and well-tested processes that are maintained in a structured, strategic environment that is a system that supports the vision.

This leads to the insight that vision-based leadership is a system, as is the more traditionally structured views of systems that are linked to infrastructure and operational mechanics in order to support physical processes. Leadership should be viewed and treated as a systematic process for movement towards the ever-evolving vision. From a leadership perspective, they should have a personal or academic process for developing the vision and aligning the organisation to it. Then they should have the plans, actions, and measurements in place to navigate the vision with all the resources and support mechanisms that the leader can manage within the scarce resources that are problematic with having a great vision and far-reaching goals.

I have always wondered what comes first, the process or the system; it's like the case of the chicken or the egg. In this discussion, I believe that effective leaders have a strategy and process to develop a vision and engage it in the organisation. The system for developing a vision requires a set of processes that involves and engages stakeholders at all levels for the effective and efficient payback to all beneficiaries.

BENEFICIARIES

THERE ARE STRATEGIC AND organic beneficiaries from good leadership and strategy. Some have strong expectations such as shareholders, whereas many others may not even recognise the fact that communities, the environment, and third parties benefit from economic growth. There is an essential element of leadership to recognising and working with beneficiaries in creating stronger benefits in a collaborative way. Suppliers are an excellent example of where both organisations benefit greatly in recognising and strategically developing growth.

I have had remarkable success working with multiple organisations in fostering cooperation and strategic purpose along the value chain to deliver continuous and constant customer benefit. When their beneficiaries are beneficial, you will find that they are stronger contributors and supporters of the strategy and the organisation's vision. A question for good leadership is recognising and communicating the shared value for their beneficiaries and creating more of them.

EMPOWERMENT

L EADERSHIP REQUIRES EMPOWERMENT FOR the teams to get on with the processes of achieving the strategy and organisational success. Empowerment requires very clear direction and rules, feedback on performance and the organisation's position, and the constant tracking of performance towards the vision.

As is mostly the case, successful behaviour is emulated, and the leader needs to have a consistent behaviour in clearly articulating expectations, providing necessary resources, and supporting empowerment through all functions and projects. Not only celebrating examples of contribution from empowered decisions but also calling out those that are not firstly a learning experience without ridicule of the individual or team requires ground-level leadership without becoming involved in day-to-day management functions. Again, the emphasis is on the individual and their team. If there are recurring issues from empowered teams, then the leader has not given the correct directions and rules, or the person or the team is inadequate. The leader never has the luxury to abdicate any responsibility or accountability for overall performance or for not taking corrective actions.

Information and its communication are crucial for keeping all the teams motivated and collaborating for optimum result. There are certain confidentialities that need to be abided by for the various audiences that the leader needs to deal with, but where information can be disseminated timely, it will build trust and engagement amongst teams.

Empowerment can be a very organic phenomenon in organisations that have clear roles, objectives, and timely and understandable feedback, with clear parameters for responsibility and chains of command.

The leader needs to take advantage of high performers through focused empowerment and acknowledge and resource the 20 per cent who will make the most headway towards the vision and advocate the strategic process. The leader cannot afford the democracy game, playing for popularity as a façade of support—and hence delivering mediocre performance. Popularity will come from success because performing organisations have positive results and belief in their direction. Empowerment should be an overall strategy in the culture and provide an overall empowered operating environment. Focussing on the few who deliver is a strategy if they have the empowerment and resources to achieve for all if benefits are distributed appropriately and development programs are in place to enable further contribution from all.

However, the leader must be able to exercise control with a controlled force that ensures tangible and intangible benefits within its teams to achieve all goals. There lies the conundrum of how deep and over what span the leader becomes involved. Not only providing resources, development, and training of teams but also ensuring morale and motivation is sufficient to the vision and its objectives. The executive management support teams are critical in keeping the leader focused and mindful to address changes that align with the organisation's growth, level of performance, and progress towards the vision.

SUCCESSION

S UCCESSION IS ALL ABOUT continuity and growth. It is not necessarily simply moving forward on the same strategic platforms. Over time, there needs to be innovation and exploitation of the organisation's continuous improvement, capability, and capacity.

Often the effort is placed on whom to hand over the mantle to rather than making sure that the business will benefit seamlessly from changes in leadership. The leader needs to ensure that the strategy is deeply embedded within the support and operating structures, the culture of the business, and the way that it interacts with all stakeholders and its community. Leaders provide resource, but it is the innovative systems that separate the business from its competitors and beneficiaries.

Succession is often thought of as a HR issue, but it should be a vital aspect of the business strategy in building sustainable systems and a culture that accepts leadership change without throwing away all the positive leadership and operational learning.

Successful leadership will have a time span, as any role does, but this is based on the competency and capabilities that the leader's tenure has delivered. The tenure may overstay the capacity of the leader in terms of where he has led the organisation to while creating a new position that is impacted by its size, geography, technology, and external forces such as political and market shifts. Therefore leaders are subject to context changes and may go the way of the dinosaur if they are unable to positively adapt.

POLITICS

THE CONFLICT AND BENEFITS of understanding politics are understanding and acknowledging people's beliefs, their aspirations, and their perception, whether based on facts or on hyped-up analysis based on what is said and what is done.

If political issues do not exist in your organisation, it is because they are not being acknowledged, which creates the greater issue of not dealing with them before they cause issues or highjack the strategy and envisioned culture of the organisation.

Politics can be positive and negative. Positive political behaviours are normally transparent and therefore are not an issue. The negative political behaviours working against the strategy or the leader are, by their nature, easily overlooked and often ignored with the flawed optimism that they will align in time.

The leader is responsible for shaping the views and cultural landscape of the organisation through influence or forceful control mechanisms that may be a harsh reality of leadership.

RESPECT

LEADERSHIP IS NOT ABOUT being comfortable or popular. It must have purpose and wide-ranging benefits, although being popular can certainly be a benefit. Leadership is all about delivering change, and change is not something that is easily accepted without an immediate or recognised benefit being seen by those who are required to change or accept it. In the end, leadership is a very disruptive process and does and will create tension.

Every change will affect people, and it is important to respect the roles and individuals that have contributed to having the organisation in a position for change to be considered. Every individual will have some contribution to affect the strategy no matter how small, but each contribution is important and hopefully leads to synchronicity of successful strategy execution.

Respect is different than being liked. Respect will come from what you do and the benefits that you bring to the table, rather than short-term charismatic activities to enlist support by being liked.

INFLUENCE

INFLUENCING HIGH ACHIEVERS AND their teams is not a challenge of perceptually being better than them. It's inspiring belief that they can stretch and have the confidence to collaborate across the organisation as required. Having hire and fire control is powerful, but it's not the most motivational tool for inspiring managers and their teams to become great. The leader must have the trust of the organisation, and this needs to be earned through the behaviour and style of the leader, as well as the performance of the organisation to the benefit of those who have an impact on the leader's tenure.

The leader may have expert power which is more in line with the expectation that the expertise will be enough to lead and nurture the organisation to its great vision. Expertise can be acquired by leading expert teams, and this requires high emotional intelligence in understanding how to influence such individuals and teams, as well as how to have diverse groups collaborating with a common purpose. Organisations are social networks, and the leader will have inherent skills on managing and developing them.

LEARNING TOOLS

P ROACTIVE ATTITUDES ARE A prerequisite to learning and progressive improvement, which are crucial to achieving newness in the organisation and its continuous journey to its evolving vision. An organisation needs to continually renew in order to enable its ongoing success and growth. Renewal programs can be driven from financial stimulus and technology, but people will always be the constant. These teams need to be continually reviewed and supported to ensure that they are consistent to the organisation's current and aspirational positions.

Training, development, and learning at all levels should be a high strategic intent within the organisation. A leader needs the best contemporary human resources to take advantage of and optimise current and future opportunities with which the organisation must deal.

The focus is on people with a broad spectrum of experiential and learning opportunities.

THE NEW HOOD

C OLLECTIVE LEADERSHIP, NOT MANAGEMENT, is required to mobilise an organisation and galvanise the support of the hoods. All levels of team managers need to be coached to become performance leaders, with all sub-leaders aligned with the visioned leader. In preparing analysis, it is often a challenge to make sense of multivariate analysis. We can draw an analogy of this because leaders need to have multivariate leadership skills when leading collectives of managers.

A new digital world now exists. Being informed or misinformed is simple and easy, and information and its analysis can be manipulated for good or bad. We are now data saturated, and this data gathering may create disorganisation and procrastination regarding making decisions to keep moving forward. Social networks have wide-reaching audiences and should not be ignored. This new way of communicating needs to be clearly understood by marketing executives, and leaders should see it as a forceful medium to sell the vision and communicate strategy and performance. Social media at all levels can get out of hand and be untruthful; this is now a critical function for the leader to manage in order to ensure the organisation is rightly informed and presented. This drives the argument of confidentiality versus the power of open information and ensuring that information, regardless of its source, is dealt with using integrity and timely correction.

There is also a transparency emerging where there are more diverse groups and subcultures within the community of the businesshood. In recognising that there is more diversity than ever, thought-directed leadership can be targeted to ensure that all contributors and threats to the strategy are not overlooked.

Communication management and all of it media are becoming a critical trait requirement and tool for effective leadership over a greater number of functions and direct and indirect support areas to the organisation. The requirement for greater management and required specialisation requires that a leader is more strategically aligned to the vision rather than the effective management of processes and systems. The focus should be on moving the spirit and beliefs of the organisation by providing support and excitement to the achievement of a high vision.

LEADING

L EARNING LEADERSHIP IS ALL about making yourself and your teams better, developing individuals, supporting the hood with bold and realisable goals, and rewarding their achievements. Unlike many aspects of study and skill acquirement, leadership is not an individual excel; it's finding the ability to group skills and individuals together to achieve greatness. "A champion team will always beat a team of champions." Successful leadership requires remarkable individual skill and knowledge, as well as human insightfulness to make individuals and teams constantly develop and excel while there is achievement of the once-believed unattainable.

Leaders lead through learning and capitalising on every opportunity to bring about actions that achieve their vision. I need to emphasise that the vision is to be a shared one, either through its inception or because it has been embedded into the organisation's culture.

Execution is multifaceted and is applied on many fronts that need to be coordinated and timely in the achievement of objectives in an efficient and effective manner. This is considerate to the capabilities of individuals, teams, and collaborative stakeholders.

Leadership is a double-edged sword. One side is the current performance and rewarding all invested interests, and the other is preparing the platform for successive leadership and vision. This is the biggest conflict that a leader can have. Too much weighting to the future objectives at the detriment to current performance expectations could jeopardise their leadership position. Time is the greatest ally and enemy, and people are the greatest resource and companions through their journey.

There is no prescription or end to leadership. It's a continuum in changes of contexts with wonderful challenges and the greatest opportunities to develop and reward people.

A leader needs to have voice, and the following points should figure in one's thoughts and strategy when thinking about one's leadership strategy. My vision with this book is to share my insights, open discussion, and generate further thoughts on leadership and its place in all hoods. I hope that it has helped you find your leader's voice and provided benefit to your hoods—and as a consequence, created many benefits for you.

- Vision

- Organisation

- Innovation

- Culture

- Execution

When not sure, go high!